Gaian Tarot

About the Author

Joanna Powell Colbert (Washington State) is an artist and writer known internationally for her goddess portraits and mythic art. She teaches workshops and e-courses on earth-centered spirituality, manifesting dreams, and tarot as a tool for inner guidance and self-exploration. The Gaian Tarot combines her love of symbolic art and the natural world, and was nine years in the making.

Visit her websites at www.gaiantarot.com and www.gaiansoul.com.

Joanna Powell Colbert

Gaian
Tarot

Llewellyn Publications
Woodbury, Minnesota

First Edition
First Printing, 2011

Book designed by Steffani Sawyer
Book edited by Laura Graves
Cover art-background swirl: © iStockphoto.com / Stanislav Pobytov
Cover design by Lisa Novak

Llewellyn Publications is a registered trademark of Llewellyn Worldwide Ltd.

ISBN: 978-0-7387-1891-0
Part of the *Gaian Tarot Kit* consisting of a deck and book.

Llewellyn Worldwide Ltd. does not participate in, endorse, or have any authority or responsibility concerning private business transactions between our authors and the public.

All mail addressed to the author is forwarded but the publisher cannot, unless specifically instructed by the author, give out an address or phone number.

Any Internet references contained in this work are current at publication time, but the publisher cannot guarantee that a specific location will continue to be maintained. Please refer to the publisher's website for links to authors' websites and other sources.

Llewellyn Publications
A Division of Llewellyn Worldwide Ltd.
2143 Wooddale Drive
Woodbury, MN 55125-2989
www.llewellyn.com

Printed in the United States of America

The Gaian Tarot is dedicated
to my beautiful granddaughter, Gracie,
and to the island that is my heart's home.

Contents

Thank You . . .

To the Tarot community for massive encouragement and support over the past ten years. To Janet Berres, who was the first person to tell me I had to create a Tarot deck. To Mary K. Greer and Teresa Michelsen, whose teachings on the Tarot are woven inextricably into this deck. To Barbara Moore for her enthusiasm and support for this project. To Ruth Ann and Wald Amberstone for producing the Readers Studio every year, and to Thalassa for producing BATS, where Tarot aficionados can congregate, meet each other, and support each other's work. To Beth Owl's Daughter and James Wells, whose insights into the Gaian Tarot have deeply enriched it. To my blog readers and Facebook friends who offered their perspectives on each card as I posted it and gave me new understanding of the meanings of the cards.

To my mermaid sisters and brothers of the Circle of Stella Maris, for being my family of choice, and for cheering me on as this project unfolded over the years—especially to Nora Cedarwind Young, Elaine Nichols, and Debra Storm for special soul-sister support. To Lunaea Weatherstone and the Sisterhood of the Silver Grove for loving encouragement. To the Friday night island sisters circle for holding the vision and for keeping it real.

To the Lummi Island community, both human and non-human, for being the matrix from which this deck emerged. To Chris Chisholm and Nikki Van Schyndel for being my naturalist mentors.

Deepest thanks to my beloved husband, Craig Olson, for his unfailing love and support, and for being willing to model for half a dozen cards on a moment's notice.

Introduction to
the Gaian Tarot

Although the first tarot cards were created in fifteenth-century northern Italy, they embody a set of spiritual principles that are timeless. In her book *The Forest of Souls*, Rachel Pollack writes that the tarot is a book of wisdom like the Bible, Torah, and other sacred texts.[1] Gaia—the living earth—is another kind of sacred text, especially for those who practice an earth-centered spirituality. I have brought together these two loves of mine—the tarot and the natural world—in the Gaian Tarot.

---

1. Rachel Pollack, *The Forest of Souls: A Walk Through the Tarot* (St. Paul, MN: Llewellyn, 2002.)

The Meaning of "Gaian"

Gaia is the primal Greek goddess who embodies the earth. The ancients saw her as the mother goddess who gave birth to the sky, sea, mountains, and the rest of creation. The sense that the earth is our "mother" is not unique to the Greeks; it is found in many indigenous cultures worldwide. In our own modern society, we know her colloquially as "Mother Nature."

In 1969 people around the world first saw that famous photo of the Earth taken from space. There was a collective emotional response to it that led to the upsurge of support for the first Earth Day and the fledgling environmental movement. The British scientist James Lovelock was inspired by the photograph, too: "The vision of that splendid white-flecked blue sphere stirred us all … There is nothing unusual in the idea of life on Earth interacting with the air, sea, and rocks, but it took a view from outside to glimpse the possibility that this combination might consist of a single giant living system."[2] Lovelock's hypothesis, simply stated, is that life on earth functions as a single, self-regulating organism. He named his hypothesis after the Greek goddess Gaia.

Lovelock's ideas were quite controversial in the scientific community, partly because of his tendency to use language that anthropomorphized the earth. His

---

2. James Lovelock, "What is Gaia?", www.ecolo.org/lovelock/what_is_ Gaia.html.

collaborator Lynn Margulis distanced herself from the personification of Gaia as a living being, preferring the image of an ecosystem of ecosystems.[3] But it is undeniable that the Gaia Hypothesis—the idea that the earth is a living (dare we say sentient?) being—fired up the imaginations of millions of people.

Whether the name Gaia is used as a poetic metaphor or as a name for an aspect of the Divine, the term "Gaian" is commonly used today to refer to a worldview that honors the earth as sacred. People who practice a Gaian spirituality understand that humans, plants, animals, stones, and stars are all inextricably linked. When we pull on one strand, it affects the whole web. We waste fuel idling our cars, and the ice in Greenland melts. DDT is outlawed in the United States and the bald eagle comes back from the brink of extinction. "Gaians" understand that the way we live our lives each day makes a difference to the rest of the world.

To practice a Gaian or earth-centered spirituality means to both give and receive spiritual sustenance from the natural world. Many of us believe that the Divine is imminent in nature and not transcendent or separate from it. Modern Gaians have much in common with the animistic worldviews of indigenous peoples. "The earth is our mother," the contemporary

---

3. Lynn Margulis, *Symbiotic Planet: A New Look at Evolution* (New York: Basic Books, 1998).

chant goes. "She will take care of us—we must take care of her."[4]

Creating the Gaian Tarot

This deck has been a long time in the making. The seed for it was planted in the 1980s when I was working with the Motherpeace Tarot and comparing it to traditional decks. I wanted to create my own deck back then, but the thought of creating seventy-eight separate pieces of artwork was daunting. I worked with the tarot consistently until the late 1990s, after which I set it aside for several years. During that time I moved to a small island and the focus of my spiritual practice changed. I began to spend much more time outside, observing the place where I lived and practicing wilderness-awareness techniques. Just like I had thrown myself into goddess studies and tarot studies, I soon became immersed in studying the native plants, birds, and animals of my chosen home. I gardened, became involved in the local community, and built a straw bale home with my husband.

When I took up the tarot again, it was with a new focus and new energy. I felt called to create my own deck. As I meditated on the meaning of each card and the fresh interpretation I might bring to it, I asked these questions: What about the earth? What does the

---

4. A traditional Native American chant popularized by the women's choral group Libana on their 1986 recording *A Circle is Cast*.

voice of the earth have to say? Where is nature in the meaning of this card?

The Gaian Tarot grew out of my relationship with the natural world where I live and the people in my neighborhood and spiritual community. Many of the scenes in the deck are based on sketches from my nature journals and photos I've taken of local landscapes. Almost every animal, bird, or plant in the cards is one I have encountered personally in my naturalist studies. I know their natural history as well as their mythic resonances—Raven and Coyote are not only mythic tricksters but also neighbors. Most of the models for the figures in my cards are friends or friends of friends. I've always loved painting the "numinous" in the everyday person, and that's what I've done here. The human figures in the deck are both contemporary and mythic, in terms of clothing and appearance. Sometimes they are part of this world, sometimes they belong in the spirit world, and sometimes they inhabit the borderlands between the two.

In total, it took me nine years to complete the artwork and companion book for the Gaian Tarot.

Tarot Structure

I have remained faithful to traditional tarot structure in the Gaian Tarot, although I have renamed many cards. There are seventy-eight cards in a deck, twenty-two of which make up the major arcana. (*Arcana* is a Latin word that means secrets or mysteries. It's related to the word "arcane.") In the tarot, the major arcana is the suit of spirit. This is where we find the deep soul lessons of our lives.

The rest of the deck, called the minor arcana, more closely resembles a deck of regular playing cards with four suits of cards from aces through kings. The suits correspond to the four elements—Air, Fire, Water, and Earth. Instead of using images of swords, wands, cups, and coins as found in most traditional tarot decks, I've used items associated with each element. In the suit of Air (traditionally the swords), I've depicted feathers, clouds, birds, butterflies, flutes, pens, and books. In the suit of Fire (wands), we'll find torches, candles, bonfires, and hearths. Water (cups) brings us rivers, fish, rain, beaches, shells, boats, and wells. Earth (pentacles or discs) is illustrated with gardens, forests, mammals, crafts, coins, and drums.

I've also made changes to the traditional "court" cards. Instead of reflecting the nobility of Renaissance Europe, these cards correspond to the stages of life: childhood, early adulthood, midlife, and old age. The traditional pages have become children and the knights have become explorers. Queens are now guardians and kings are elders. There are two males and two females in each category, which is also different from the traditional tarot where queens are always female and kings are always male. The children symbolize the qualities of discovery and birth. Explorers seek challenges and embody the principle of growth. The guardians are productive and involved in the community; they represent the concept of fruition. Elders give counsel and stand for the qualities of dissemination and decay.

The design on the back of the cards shows a wreath of blessing herbs—cedar, sage, sweetgrass, and lavender. It is the same wreath seen on the World card, set against the sky from the Star card. The wreath creates a doorway or portal between this world and the Otherworld.

Using the Deck and Book

There are as many ways to work with tarot cards as there are people who use them. Some people like to pull a card each morning and reflect on how its theme might appear in the day to come. Some people use the cards as writing prompts in journaling for self-exploration. Others use them as inspiration for wildly creative projects or brainstorming sessions. Some play games. And some use the cards as an oracle, a way of accessing divine guidance, whether this guidance is perceived as coming from God/dess (the Great Mystery) or from the deep Self.

Every tarot card has a spectrum of meaning, from positive to negative. If you like to read reversed cards, you would read the shadow (or negative) side of the card I've provided in the card descriptions when a reversed card turns up.

If you choose not to read reversed cards, the shadow side of the cards still comes into play in challenging positions in a spread, such as "challenge," "what not to do," "what is harmful," etc. You'll know when to read the shadow side as you gain experience working with the cards.

When used for divination, the tarot can be viewed as a spiritual weathervane. It can tell you which way the wind is blowing in your life at a given moment. But only you can set your sail and choose your course.

I hope that the Gaian Tarot helps you to connect with the Divine, in whatever way you conceive that to be. I hope you will be inspired to connect more deeply with the natural world in the place where you live. And I hope my images help create a culture of strong and gentle women and men, working together to create a beautiful, peaceful and just planet.

The Major Arcana:
Soul Lessons

We shall not cease from exploration
And the end of all our exploring
Will be to arrive where we started
And know the place for the first time.

–T. S. Eliot, *The Four Quartets*

The mythic figure of the traveler, explorer, or vagabond has a strong pull on our hearts and minds. Who
among us has not longed to "light out for the territo-
ries" like Huck Finn, or hit the road like Jack Kerouac,
or embark on a dangerous yet exciting mission like
Frodo and Samwise?

The stories of such journeys speak to us because
they are metaphors for our own life journeys. The
quest is "the oldest story in the world … it must be told
time and time again so that we never forget why we are
on Earth and what we have to do here."[5]

---

5. Hajo Banzhaf, *Tarot and the Journey of the Hero* (York Beach, ME: Samuel
    Weiser, 2000),17.

The path through the major arcana is one such symbolic journey. The sequence of these twenty-two cards has been called the Fool's Journey, the Hero's Journey, and the Heroine's Journey. In the Gaian Tarot, it is the Seeker's Journey. Whether we act the role of fool, seeker, hero, or heroine, we are each on a quest to become our deepest, most authentic selves.

The cards and characters of the major arcana represent twenty-two soul lessons and archetypes which grew out of the religious and mystical worldview of Renaissance Europe. These "soul lessons" clearly have universal appeal, as they have lasted and thrived to the present day.

The figures on the major cards are mysterious, seductive characters who draw us in—we want to know their secrets. The majors have also been called trumps or keys. The word "trump" derives from the word "triumph," and refers not only to the allegorical parades of the Italian Renaissance (the *trionfi*) and the suit of trump cards in *tarocchi* and bridge, but also to the soul's triumph over adversity. And a key, of course, unlocks a door, a treasure chest, or a secret. In *The Forest of Souls*, Rachel Pollack suggests that an alternative interpretation of "keys" is the keys on a piano. We can play beautiful music of our own devising on the tarot keys, once we have learned what each key does.

In most decks, the first card of the major arcana—the Fool—is pictured as a traveler of some kind. The person is a tramp following a path, oblivious to the cat or dog trying to get his or her attention. Or the Fool is a court jester who nearly steps off a cliff because he isn't looking where he's going. Or she's a girl stepping off a cliff onto a rainbow bridge, with complete trust that all will be well. In the Gaian Tarot, the Seeker is a young woman pausing on the edge of a cliff, gazing at the beautiful landscape below before setting out on her adventure.

We will join the Seeker on her journey through the major arcana. We will unlock doors, play beautiful melodies, and come to know ourselves a little better. The characters we will meet invite us to live our lives on a mythic level, reminding us that there is a sacred purpose in everything we do.

0 · The Seeker
(The Fool)

A New Beginning

The Seeker begins a journey, taking a moment to contemplate the road ahead before setting off down the hillside. Perhaps she is murmuring a prayer or setting an intention. She travels lightly, carrying all she needs in her bundle. She has embroidered a butterfly on the back of her vest, signifying her delight in taking wing and setting out on her own path.

A great mountain rises in the east, and the river slowly meanders on its own journey from the mountain range to the bay and the ocean beyond.

The Seeker is at that stage of life between childhood and adulthood when anything is possible—her life lies before her like a page waiting to be written. With Fox as her trickster companion, who knows what surprises await? Swallows and swallowtails flit and flutter around her, guiding her way.

When you get this card in a reading...

You are starting a new journey with a beginner's mind. It's time to hit the road—metaphorically or literally. Every time you set out on a journey, whether it's a one-day hike or a new career, you embark on a spiritual journey as well. Be open to all the twists and curves in the road ahead. Be ready for wonderful surprises. Keep your heart open and maintain an attitude of innocence, trust, and spontaneity. Remember that many innovators, creators, and explorers were considered foolish by the conventional wisdom of their time. Dare to take a risk! Before you is a brand-new adventure—the chance for a fresh start and endless possibilities.

When you read the Shadow side of this card...

Are you longing to hit the road, escape, or seek more adventure in your life, but are afraid to do it? Maybe responsibilities are holding you back and it seems like the wrong time to take a risk. Do you fear you have too much to lose? On the other hand, you may be too nonchalant, like a vagabond or an immature adult who refuses to grow up. It may be time to become more serious and settled. Be careful of a tendency to be naive or gullible. Are you being wise or foolish about your current situation?

Deepen Your Understanding of the Seeker

THEMES

- Spiritual quest
- Innocence/childlike wonder
- Pilgrimage
- New beginnings
- The wisdom of the fool

- Spontaneity
- Simplicity
- Adventure
- Taking a risk
- Alpha/omega

SYMBOLS

White feather in hair: Purity, innocence, soul-flight.

Bundle with talismans: Her "baggage" and the prayers/hopes/aspirations she carries on the pilgrimage.

Walking stick: Helps her over the rough patches; something to lean on. May be a magic wand in disguise, a branch of the world tree that connects heaven and earth.

Mountain: Spiritual ascent, clear uncluttered mind, high ideals, peak experience, meeting place of heaven and earth (yang).

Valley: Fertility, cultivation, home (yin).

River: Boundary between one world and another; passage through various worlds; going with the flow; purification; refreshment.

Tree: Tree of life, world tree *(axis mundi),* connects three realms: underworld, middle world, celestial world.

Birds: Messengers between heaven and earth; soul-flight, freedom.

Swallows: Harbinger of summer, a good time for a journey.

Butterflies: Lightness, joy, transformation, metamorphosis, symbol of the soul.

Fox: A trickster in southwestern Native American tradition; a shapeshifter in Chinese mythology. Blends in with surroundings, signifying stealth, cunning, and camouflage. Often seen at the borderlines of dawn and twilight; can be a guide to the Otherworld.

JOURNAL QUESTIONS

What journey do I begin today?

How can I cultivate beginner's mind?

How can I be more childlike?

Have I lost my sense of wonder? How can I reconnect with it?

Where or how in my life do I feel foolish? Is this my perception or the judgment of others?

Where or how do I need to lighten up?

What grand adventure would I like to have?

Where do I need to take a risk?

What is shapeshifting (changing shape) in my life?

What am I carrying in my bundle? Is my baggage light or heavy?

How can I simplify my life?

What kind of healing does the Seeker offer me?

What kind of healing can I offer the earth
through the example of the Seeker?

AFFIRMATION
I make my life a walking prayer.

1 · The Magician

Spirit Made Manifest

The Magician is a ritual drummer, the drum his magic wand. He plays the djembe, caught up in the bliss and ecstasy of the trance created by the sound of the drum. He knows that the rhythm of his drumbeat matches the earth's heartbeat. Firelight flickers on cave walls, painted with a thousand hands, like the prehistoric handprints in the Cueva de las Manos (Cave of the Hands) in Argentina. An altar with items representing the four elements anchors him in sacred space. He creates the matrix that allows magic to happen. He opens a door between this world and the world of Spirit. The hand creates magic—whether with a drum, paintbrush, or ritual tool. Hands bring the unseen into the realm of the seen.

When you get this card in a reading…
You have the power to manifest your desires. Charisma and personal energy radiate from you. It is your gift to be able to enter sacred space and bring spiritual energy into the world of matter. When you focus your will,

passion, and joy, creative energy flows through you. It is not enough to have focus and intention; you know these must be followed by action! Your creativity energizes you and blesses those around you. Align yourself with the heartbeat of the earth, and bring forth healing for the planet and all her creatures. Make things happen.

When you read the Shadow side of this card ...
Your creative energies are blocked. Is this due to low self-esteem or an inability to focus? In what ways might you be refusing to step into your power or to take responsibility for your life? Sometimes an overconfident attitude may be hiding a secret lack of confidence. Beware of the temptation to behave unethically to get your way or to impose your will upon others. You may be stuck in self-limiting beliefs. Will you choose to remain stuck, or will you do whatever it takes to free yourself and let the energy flow once again?

Deepen Your Understanding of the Magician

THEMES

- Empowerment
- Focused intent
- Creative energy
- Ideas become reality
- Action
- Yang in contrast to the Priestess's yin
- Will
- Magic
- Skill
- Manifestation
- Ecstasy

Symbols

Hands: Manifestation, creativity, giving and receiving, personal expression, energizing touch of God/dess.

Drum or drumming: Rhythm of divine creation, heartbeat, ecstasy, trance, taking action, summoning up magic powers.

Fire: Transformation and destruction, life force, energy.

Cave: Womb of Mother Earth, gestation, cauldron of creativity, initiation into deep mysteries.

Four Elements (altar, necklace): The building blocks of creation, the full circle, wholeness, the four suits of the tarot.

Sun (on drumhead): Strength, vitality, energy, joy.

Red and white flowers (on vest): Passion and purity, earth and spirit, yin and yang.

Red (pants): Passion, blood, life force, willpower, courage, sensuality.

Lemniscate (infinity sign): Never-ending flow between heaven and earth, spirit and matter. A link to the Strength card.

Journal Questions

How do I express my own sense of personal power?

Where in my life do I need to focus my will and take action?

Do I manifest my desires in a responsible way?

Do I impose my will upon others?

How does magic flow through me?

How do I express my creativity?

*When do I feel like I am channeling spiritual
energy into a physical form?*

What is my greatest skill?

What skills do I need to improve?

What new creative medium might I try?

*When do I feel like I am aligned with
the heartbeat of the Earth?*

What kind of healing does the Magician offer me?

*What kind of healing can I offer the earth
through the example of the Magician?*

AFFIRMATION

I have the power to manifest my desires.

2 · The Priestess
(The High Priestess)

Dreams, Voices, Visions

The woman of mystery calls upon us to turn within when the moon is waning. Listen, she says, to the voice of the wind with its pungent, salty scent...listen to the voices that arise in your dreams or from your womb during the time of moonflow.

She sits before the willow veil of Hecate and hears the unspoken words of Owl and Salmon; the sea behind her is illuminated by a waning moon. At her side is the Sleeping Goddess of Malta, who sends healing dreams. In her hands is the rubyfruit of Persephone, a symbol of fertility, death, and sexuality.

Is she Maiden? Is she Crone? She carries both within her, balancing the wisdom of age with the freshness of youth—and holds fast to the autonomy of both.

Shh—the priestess whispers:

Guard the mysteries! Constantly reveal them!

When you get this card in a reading…

It is time to go within and develop non-linear, non-rational ways of knowing. Pay close attention to your dreams, as they may carry potent messages for you. Let your intuition flow. Listen for the subtext in others' words; hear the words they don't speak out loud. Watch for synchronicities and omens in your everyday life. Study the "dark arts" of divination—reading the cards or the stars, scrying, or interpreting dreams. Listen for voices in the wind, look for patterns in the clouds. Meditate. Study the language of symbol and myth. At the dark of the moon or (if you are a woman) when your wise blood flows, listen to the still, small voice within. It is the Priestess's voice—it speaks of mysteries, secrets, and truth.

When you read the Shadow side of this card…

Someone may be denying or devaluing nonlinear, "irrational" ways of knowing. It is unwise to squelch your intuition and dishonor your feelings. Are you ignoring your dreams and the messages they bring?

You or someone important to you may be caught up in delusion or illusion or spending too much time in otherworldly reality. Perhaps it is time to emerge from seclusion, reveal secrets, and be more active in the world once again.

Deepen Your Understanding of the Priestess

Themes

- Non-rational ways of knowing
- Dreams
- Moods, emotions
- Privacy
- Listening to your inner voice
- Yin in contrast to the Magician's yang
- Inner, esoteric teachings in contrast to the Teacher's outer, exoteric teachings
- Trusting intuitive wisdom
- Secrets
- Spiritual purpose
- Autonomy
- Memory
- Women's (menstrual) mysteries
- Solitude

Symbols

Willow: Sacred to Hecate, the old one, the wise woman. The "weeping willow" is a symbol of grief and death in the West; in China, a symbol of immortality. Its medicinal uses include relieving pain and thinning the blood.

Veil (of willow): Hidden (or partly hidden) knowledge. Half-concealed secrets with the promise of revelation.

Pomegranate: Emblem of the maiden Persephone, also called the rubyfruit. Sexuality, fertility, death and rebirth, knowledge of good and evil, loss of innocence. Also symbolizes women's mysteries: the womb, blood, childbearing. Pomegranates contain phytoestrogens, substances similar to our naturally produced hormone estrogen, as well as cancer-preventing antioxidants.

Dreaming Goddess of Malta: Divination and healing through dreaming. Ancient Maltese temples were constructed in the shape of a woman's body. Pilgrims came to sleep in the temple in the hope of receiving dreams that would cure their illnesses or give them divine guidance.

Salmon: Wisdom, knowledge, second sight, poetic inspiration (Celtic). Spiritual nourishment, determination, renewal (Pacific Northwest Native American).

Owl: Strength in silence (noiseless flight), night vision, guidance, wisdom. Can also symbolize death and ghosts.

Water/the sea: Feelings, emotions, the unconscious. Hidden or secret teachings. That which we cross to reach the Otherworld. Primordial soup, from which all life arises. Life/death/rebirth.

Waning moon: The Crone (third face of the Goddess), the dark mysteries. Hidden knowledge, end of cycle. Releasing and letting go.

Crescent moon (on headband): The Maiden (first face of the Goddess), the bright mysteries. Beginning of a cycle. Budding and flowering.

Spirals (on gown): Contraction and expansion, repetitive rhythm of life, cyclical nature of evolution, constant flux and movement, symbol of the soul's journey. Found in every culture.

Black and white (clothing): Yin and yang, opposites in balance.

White cross with red center (clothing): A cross symbolizes the marriage of heaven and earth, male and female, the conscious and unconscious. The Maltese cross (where the limbs of the cross are wider at the ends than at the center) directs attention to the center, the *omphalos* (navel of the earth).

JOURNAL QUESTIONS:

What do I keep hidden, private, or sacred?

Do I trust my instincts and intuition?

In what ways can I explore my inner life?

Who are the wise women in my life?
How can I learn from them?

Have I ever had psychic experiences?

What does it mean to be a priestess?

Do I have the calling to the priestess path?

What needs to be kept secret and what can I reveal?

What does my intuition tell me?

What esoteric body of knowledge do I study?

What kind of healing does the Priestess offer me?

What kind of healing can I offer the earth through the example of the Priestess?

AFFIRMATION

I know when to speak and when to keep silent.

3 · The Gardener
(The Empress)

Sensuality, Creativity, Abundance

Our Lady of the Land revels in the fertility and lushness of the midsummer fields, the first fruits of the harvest and the ripening of her own body. She is the mother Demeter, of the wheat and poppies. She is the daughter of the Great Goddess of Willendorf. She is the Monarch butterfly. She embodies Venus/Aphrodite as well, luxuriating in sensuality and eroticism. She is both mother and lover and, in proudly proclaiming her right to be both, she heals Western society's split between sexuality and motherhood.

She wears a kukui nut necklace, a Hawaiian symbol of status and empowerment. The mirror of Venus reflects her own beauty and gives us a glimpse into the Otherworld. She is surrounded by overflowing baskets of produce, as fields yet to be harvested stretch out to the horizon.

"Take and eat," she says as she offers us an apple, papaya, and fig—the fruitfulness of our own souls. "It is good."

When you get this card in a reading...

It is a time of great fertility and abundance for you. You are pregnant with new creations—an art form, book, project, perhaps even a baby. You embody both the nurturing mother and the sensual lover. You are a steward of the land which you plant, weed, and nourish in a sustainable manner. At harvest time, you offer sustenance to those you love. You are a hard worker, but you take great delight in the scent of lavender fields on a hot summer day and the dizzying riot of color, shapes, and textures in the garden. You love your own body; you love your mate, children, friends, and community. You love the natural world around you. Your appetite for connection, sensuality, and creativity seems boundless. The people around you are blessed to have you in their lives.

When you read the Shadow side of this card...

You may be experiencing infertility or a lack of abundance in your life. It may feel like the dead of winter when nothing grows, but remember that seeds are still alive, hibernating underground.

It's also possible that rampant growth is threatening to overwhelm you and needs to be pruned and cut back. You may be experiencing poor health and could be disconnected from the natural world. Do you have "nature-deficit disorder"? It's time to get out into the garden and play in the mud.

Deepen Your Understanding of the Gardener

THEMES

- Creativity
- Productivity
- Nurturing
- Passion
- Vibrant health
- Abundance
- Healing the mother/ lover split

- Fertility
- Growth
- Sensuality
- Embracing the natural world
- Appreciating beauty
- Comfort
- Motherhood

SYMBOLS

Garden: Paradise, the abode of the soul. Cultivated land, in contrast to the wilderness, must be cared for and nurtured (like one's soul or spiritual path).

Apples and Apple Tree: Tree of Life, love, fertility, desire. Emblem of Venus. Immortality, death and rebirth.

Pregnancy: Fertility, productivity, gestation.

Basket of produce, fields ready for harvest: Abundance, prosperity.

Butterflies: Lightness, joy, transformation, metamorphosis, symbol of the soul.

Butterflies mating: Sexuality.

Monarch butterfly: Queen or monarch of one's life.

Kukui nut (necklace): A Hawaiian symbol of status and empowerment.

Dolphin (necklace): From the Greco-Roman *delphinos*, from the Greek root *delphus*, meaning womb. Increased creativity, fertility. Emblem of Aphrodite.

Robin: Harbinger of spring, new growth. Successful living in almost any habitat, always depending on one another to watch for danger while communally feeding. If we pay attention, it is Robin who will consistently communicate what's happening all around us in nature.

Swallows: Harbinger of summer, height of growing season.

Rabbit: Love, fertility, menstrual cycle.

Venus glyph (shape of mirror): Love and sexuality, symbol of woman.

Wheat: Emblem of Demeter, mother of agriculture. A mother's devotion. The dying resurrected god, resurrection.

Poppies: Another emblem of Demeter; she created the poppy to aid her in sleep after grieving the loss of her daughter Persephone. Sleep, death, rebirth, eternal life.

Figs: Female sexuality, fertility, prosperity.

Papaya: Love, desire, womanhood, prosperity.

Willendorf figurine: The Great Mother. From Neolithic times, humans have associated the fertility and abundance of the Earth with the female body. Luck, wealth, pleasure.

River: Boundary between one world and another; passage through various worlds; going with the flow; purification; refreshment.

Journal Questions

What am I gestating? What waits to be born?

How do I celebrate my beauty and sensuality?

Where in my life am I experiencing abundance and prosperity?

What have I planted?

What am I harvesting?

What am I passionate about?

Is there a split between my sexual self and my nurturing, mothering self? If so, how can I heal it?

How do I care for my garden (literally or metaphorically)?

What kind of relationship do I have with the earth?

Am I eating healthy foods?

How often do I eat seasonal, local foods?

How do I connect to the place where I live?

What kind of healing does the Gardener offer me?

What kind of healing can I offer the earth through the example of the Gardener?

Affirmation

I give thanks for the abundance and prosperity in my life.

4 · The Builder
(The Emperor)

Structure, Boundaries, Foundation

The Builder is a master craftsman, shown here carving a design of oak leaves and acorns into the post that flanks the front door of his home. He is committed to the ethics and principles of sustainability and has built an earth-friendly house. Drying herbs hang from the rafters, firewood is stacked in preparation for winter, and a spiral of beach stones leads the visitor to the arched doorway.

The Builder is strong and comfortable in his own authority. Yet unlike most historic emperors, he does not destroy life for his own power or benefit. Inspired by the Green Man, the spirit of the wildwood whose face he has carved into the post, he works in harmony with nature and honors Mother Earth's animals and resources. The kestrel, a small falcon who hunts with speed, grace, and precision, watches and waits as the Builder focuses on his task.

The Builder is the archetypal Father, the creator of culture, structure, and human laws, as compared to the Gardener, who embodies the abundance of Mother Earth. He is the city, she is the country. He is the building, she is the garden. As an architect of civilization, our Builder creates networks and systems that enable people to live and work together, sharing resources and creating a supportive, sustainable community.

When you get this card in a reading...
It's time to embrace your authority. The Builder tells you that for now it is wiser to make decisions through logic and pragmatic reasoning, rather than your emotions or intuition. Ask yourself: "What am I building? Are the foundations of my life based on strong structures? Are my boundaries clear and well tended?"

You are ready to take responsibility for a project where you have authority over others. What kind of a leader are you? How might you polish your skills? Do you lead by example or by dominating? Are you secure enough to share power with others? Do you take into account the longterm consequences of decisions you make? The Builder exemplifies the Good Father who loves, guides, and protects his children. Having clear boundaries and a disciplined approach bring security.

When you read the Shadow side of this card...
This is a leader who stifles or micromanages. He or she may prefer a power-over, autocratic style of leading. Someone in authority may be too harsh or too emotional, or have trouble making decisions. Who is attempting to exploit nature for its resources, without

respect for stewardship or sustainability? Someone may be having difficulty with setting limits or boundaries, making abusive behavior possible. This may also indicate a negative attitude towards fatherhood.

Deepen Your Understanding of the Builder

THEMES

- Leadership
- Defining limits
- Masculinity
- Protector and provider
- Logic
- Rationality
- Rules
- Acting responsibly
- Administration
- Creating order
- Stability
- Authority
- Giving direction
- Fatherhood
- Intellect
- Structure
- Discipline
- Organization
- Goal-oriented
- Civilization and culture

SYMBOLS

Post/pillar: Support; an essential structural element that bears the weight of the building. The World Axis (*axis mundi*) that holds the three worlds together—the underworld, the middle world, the upper world. Two pillars indicate a gateway to knowledge.

Kestrel: A small falcon also known as a sparrowhawk. A predator who is quick, precise, and graceful. Brings the gift of making swift, discriminating choices.

Hammer and chisel: A hammer can both create and destroy, depending on how it's used. By itself it is a crude instrument, but it becomes precise when used with a chisel. The hammer can be seen as willpower and the chisel as discernment.

Green Man: The spirit inherent in trees, plants, and foliage; male fertility in nature.

Drying herbs: Good stewardship; providing medicine for the household.

Firewood: Good stewardship; providing warmth for the winter ahead; knowing which trees make the best logs and are easiest to burn (woodcraft).

Doorway: A barrier; an initiate must have a key to pass through it; an opportunity or transition; threshold, liminality; the passage from one state of being to another.

House: The center of your world. In dreams, it represents your life, inner being, or belief system.

Spiral: Contraction and expansion, repetitive rhythm of life, cyclical nature of evolution, constant flux and movement, symbol of the soul's journey.

Oak leaves: The Celtic Oak King, symbol of the waxing year. Strength, longevity, height of one's power (spiritual and material). Oak is a great building wood, its acorns are one of the most nutritional foods in nature, and the tannins leached out of acorns before consumption include medicinal and utilitarian chemicals.

Building: A microcosm of the universe. In dreams, different floors of a building correspond to different states of consciousness. The main floor is the conscious mind, the basement is the unconscious; the upper floor is the superconscious, or connection to the Divine.

The act of building: Assimilating new beliefs, creating a new or different state of consciousness.

Journal Questions

What am I building?

What needs structure in my life?

Are my boundaries strong and in place?

What kind of a leader am I?

What is my style of leadership?

How do I feel about sharing power with others?

How am I acting responsibly?

How am I creating culture?

How do I create sustainability?

What did my own father teach me?
  How am I like/unlike him?

What kind of healing does the Builder offer me?

What kind of healing can I offer the earth
  through the example of the Builder?

Affirmation

I wield my power with wisdom based on my discipline, knowledge, and respect for all that is.

5 · The Teacher
(The Hierophant)

Learning and Teaching

The Teacher is a humble and spiritual figure in the tradition of the Holy Fool or Crazy Saint, known in Sufi tradition as well as in Christianity, Tibetan Buddhism, and Hasidic Judaism. Crazy saints speak in riddles, tease, laugh uproariously, and act intentionally ridiculous. At the same time, they are guileless, transparent, and open to a sense of wonder.

The Teacher sits in front of a Western Red Cedar surrounded by five green allies, potent medicinal herbs that many would pass by as weeds. Is it crazy to take as your teachers Dandelion, Stinging Nettle, Garlic, Yarrow, and Comfrey? And what lessons are taught by Western Red Cedar?

Coyote is a crazy saint as well. Many wilderness awareness teachers pass on the tradition of "coyote teaching," in which they use methods like questioning, teasing, and storytelling to inspire and intrigue lazy students. Coyote teaching also happens when you plan to learn one thing (the medicinal use of herbs, for example) and end up learning something else altogether (perhaps the limits of your own courage and stamina).

Who, we may ask, is the Teacher in this card, and who is the student?

When you get this card in a reading...

This card may signal the arrival of a spiritual teacher in your life—or you may be ready to become a teacher to others. It may be that this teacher will appear in disguise—the weeds that grow along the roadside, or a heron feeding in the mud flats at low tide. The natural world around you has some of the most profound spiritual teachings you will ever encounter. Perhaps it is time to get to know your place on this earth in a more intimate manner. Do you know the names of native plants in your area and how the indigenous people use them? Do you know how to interpret the different calls and songs of the birds in your neighborhood? Do you know where the sun rises and sets on the horizon in summer and in winter? The Teacher calls you to become intimately acquainted with the natural world in the place where you live as part of your spiritual practice.

When you read the Shadow side of this card...

Someone's belief system is inflexible, with no room for questioning or movement. Take a look at how oppressive religious structures, rigid church doctrine, or questionable guru figures (including those in the personal growth movement) may be affecting a situation. There could be a problem when someone is disconnected from the natural world and ignoring the blessings to be found there. Perhaps a call to share wisdom with the world is being ignored.

Deepen your understanding of the Teacher

THEMES

- Teaching or guiding others
- Guidance
- Counseling
- A course of study
- Education
- Spiritual teachings outside of mainstream religious institutions
- Spiritual link (priest)— intercessor
- Being taught or led
- Belief systems
- Mentor
- Search for truth
- Tradition
- Outer, exoteric teachings in contrast to the Priestess's inner, esoteric teachings
- Revealing the sacred to the light of day

SYMBOLS

Tree: The Tree of Life appears in cross-cultural mythology as a symbol of fertility or everlasting life. In science, it is a metaphor for the evolutionary interrelatedness of living things. In the Kabbalah, it is a diagram of the creation of the world. The World Tree is another cross-cultural symbol that depicts a Tree connecting the heavens, the earth, and, with its roots, the underground.

Western red cedar: The "tree of life" or "life giver" to indigenous coastal Pacific Northwest tribes, *Thuja plicata* was (and is) used for shelter, boats, clothing, hats, baskets, blankets, diapers, dishes, cooking vessels, utensils, boxes, ropes, weapons, jewelry, masks, and medicine. Groves of old-growth cedars are places of power, used for ceremonies and retreats. The Western red cedar can live to be 1,500 years old and, as such, is a symbol of long life and eternity.

Heron: A waterbird who stands motionless at the border of land and water, as if in a meditative state. Peace, serenity, grace, independence, self-reflection, a sentinel. Like all birds, a messenger between heaven and earth.

Coyote: A trickster who is feared by some and revered by others. A mediator between life and death. A paradox, creator, and teacher.

Dandelion: A weed to many, yet the greens are nourishing to the liver and contain antioxidants as well. The cheery yellow flowers signify happiness and the return of spring. When we blow on the puffball and spread its seeds, we hope for our wishes to come true.

Garlic: The "stinking rose" is reputed to have powerful antibiotic, antiviral, and antifungal properties. The many layers that create the bulb have been seen as a symbol of the unfolding cosmos. It also stands for courage and strength, and is reputed to be an aphrodisiac.

Nettles: The young leaves of stinging nettles are welcome as one of the first signs of spring. They may be symbolic of "pain but not sorrow" because the formic acid inside their stinging hairs is used to relieve arthritis, among other applications. They actually make a tasty treat, if gathered and cooked with care. Nettles are also symbolic as a "sting of strength" since their fibers have always been revered as some of the strongest for making rope, clothing, and fishing nets. Nutritionally, nettles are high in plant protein, vitamins, and minerals, especially iron.

Comfrey: Known as "heal-all," comfrey is good for soothing lungs, healing cuts and bruises, and knitting together broken bones. It is regenerative and reportedly ensures safety during travel. The comfrey plant is extremely prolific and difficult to destroy.

Yarrow: A curative for coughs and colds while also reducing fevers, it is an emblem of courage, love, and divination. It staunches the flow of blood from deep cuts. The sticks used to cast the hexagrams of the I Ching are made of yarrow.

Prayer beads: Surround the neck and throat chakra, a symbol of communication. Teaching while talking. The chanting of mantras or prayers. The commitment to a spiritual practice. Connection with all others who pray or meditate.

Bare feet: Bare feet are in touch with the earth, symbolizing a state of being well-grounded. Practical spirituality ("both feet on the ground").

Calm water: Peace, tranquillity, spiritual refreshment.

JOURNAL QUESTIONS

What do I have to teach?

What do I have to learn?

How connected am I to the place where I live?

What wisdom can the green allies offer me?

When have I experienced "coyote teaching"?

What is the place of tradition in my life?

Who is my current teacher?

What is my purpose?

What kind of healing does the Teacher offer me?

*What kind of healing can I offer the earth
through the example of the Teacher?*

AFFIRMATION

I receive my best spiritual teachings from nature.

6 · The Lovers

Follow Your Passion

The Lovers celebrate the sacred feast of Beltane (May Day) in their greenwood bower, attended by the swan of Aphrodite and her twin doves. He is resplendent as the sun, and she is green as the growing earth. He is crowned with leaves, she with mayflowers—hawthorn blossoms, which remind us to follow our bliss. Between them they hold the blood-red wild rose of summer, symbol of the sweetness and the sting of passion. A bumblebee hovers near the rose, waiting the chance to drink deeply of its nectar. For a moment, the two figures have turned away from being caught up in each other's gaze to look outward together in the same direction.

When you get this card in a reading…
It's time for you to look deeply into your own heart and ask yourself if you are living a life full of passion and love. What gives you deep joy and fulfillment in your life? Whatever it is, are you pursuing it? When you are

living an authentic life, pursuing your deepest passions, it is easy to love yourself and others.

The Beloved appears in many guises. A romantic or erotic lover, a friend, a life partner, family members, animal companions, the natural world, an art or craft or profession, God/dess—all these can be the Beloved. All these are deserving of our unconditional love. Giving and receiving love is our natural state of being.

Remember also that your sexuality is sacred in whatever way you choose to express it. "All acts of love and pleasure are my rituals," the Lady says to you. Above all, be true to yourself and behave ethically with your lovers.

Often this card appears when there is a choice to be made. The Lovers call upon you to always follow your heart's desire.

When you read the Shadow side of this card…
You may have experienced pain and disappointment in your relationship with a Beloved, which makes it challenging to give or receive love. You may be holding back or isolating yourself from others. The practice of gratitude makes our hearts expand. When we focus on all the things about our Beloved for which we are grateful instead of focusing on the qualities our Beloved lacks, our love grows. When our hearts are filled with gratitude, the ability to give unconditional love doesn't seem so difficult.

Deepen Your Understanding of the Lovers

THEMES

- Passion
- Follow your bliss
- Sexuality
- Union of opposites
- Reciprocity
- Partnership
- Self-love
- Interdependence

- Heart's desire
- Choice
- Love
- Balance
- Cooperation
- Sacred marriage
- Relationships of all kinds
- Honor the Beloved

SYMBOLS

Bower of greenery: Springtime, the life-force. A bower is a private place or a lady's bedroom.

Hawthorn: The mayflower, which blooms at Beltane. A tincture made of its berries supports blood and heart health. Your heart's desire.

Wild rose: Love, passion. Emblem of Aphrodite/Venus and Mary, symbols of divine womanhood. The five-petaled rose is related to the pentacle, a symbol of the four elements plus the element of spirit.

Rose thorns: The pain that sometimes comes along with love and passion.

Bee: Sexual fertility (pollination). The honeycomb is a hexagon, reflecting the Lovers' number, 6.

Swan: Emblem of Aphrodite, goddess of erotic love. Creature of land and water. Grace and beauty.

Doves: Another emblem of Aphrodite. Messenger, fidelity, peace, hope.

Spirals: Contraction and expansion, repetitive rhythm of life, cyclical nature of evolution, constant flux and movement, symbol of the soul's journey.

Cowrie shell necklace: The shape echoes the shape of the yoni (vulva); female sexuality.

Heart-shaped pendant: Love.

JOURNAL QUESTIONS

What are the most significant relationships in my life?

Who is the Beloved to me?

What is my relationship with Spirit (God/dess)?

What choice do I need to make?

How can I make an authentic choice?

What is my heart's passion?

How do I express my sexuality?

What or who do I love the most?

What or who would I give my heart to, if I had no fear?

What kind of healing do the Lovers offer me?

What kind of healing can I offer the earth through the example of the Lovers?

AFFIRMATION

I give and receive love joyfully and unconditionally.

7 · The Canoe
(The Chariot)

Stay Focused on Your Path

The paddler sets out on his quest, unencumbered by baggage or even excess clothing. He is focused on his goal, looking neither to the left nor right. The phrase "paddle your own canoe" indicates self-determination and self-reliance. He brings his strength, will, and courage to the task at hand. A boat often symbolizes transition from the material world to the spirit world. Here the paddler makes his way in the world while exploring spiritual depths. His task is to live his life with meaning—to infuse everyday life with his soul purpose.

His paddle is his magic wand, his tattoos his armor. His companions on the journey are Eagle and Salmon, each bringing their own gifts—swiftness, power, and keen sight from Eagle, wisdom of the deep from Salmon. The black-and-white orcas bring their own powerful magic, the balance of playfulness and fierceness. No doubt they will challenge and guide him.

When you get this card in a reading ...

This is a time to stay focused on your path, and to exercise self-discipline as you work towards your goal. Set aside anything extraneous that would distract you or keep you from completing your task. What is your goal? What do you want to accomplish? This card may apply to your life in the everyday world—pursuing a course of study, career goal, fitness plan, or creative project. It may also apply to your inner life; perhaps you are in a recovery program or are healing from a trauma. Whatever your goal, set your intention, take your first steps, and your guides and allies will be at your side to help you on your way. Have great courage! No matter how hard your journey seems, know that you have what it takes to succeed.

When you read the Shadow side of this card ...

Energy may be scattered and progress becomes difficult. Avoid spinning your wheels or being distracted from your purpose. You may have set an intention but are not taking action. Or perhaps you are pushing too hard and have lost the pleasure of the project. Opposing ideas may bring conflict. Someone may be creating trouble through unfairness or a lack of discipline, or maybe being overly aggressive in his or her tactics. At what cost does a journey of self-discovery come?

Deepen Your Understanding of the Canoe

THEMES

- Focus
- Self-discipline
- Initiation, rite of passage
- Testing yourself; endurance
- Determination
- Self-reliance, independence
- Working towards your goal
- Success, victory, triumph
- Finding (or creating) your place in the world
- An outward journey in the world that reflects an inner journey of change

SYMBOLS

Canoe: A vehicle that takes us from one place to another. A boat often symbolizes transition from the material to the spirit world. We must move under our own power, going at our own pace, in a canoe. The phrase "paddle your own canoe" indicates self-determination and self-reliance, while "pulling canoe" (with other paddlers) reflects a more tribal inter-dependency.

Traveling over water instead of land: Water is symbolic of an emotional or psychic terrain. Land is also there, represented by the island in the background. The paddler is on a spiritual quest as well as a quest to establish himself in the world.

Paddle: He has a paddle instead of a wand or scepter, both symbols of spiritual or temporal power. The paddle is inscribed with a fourfold design that draws on the power of the four directions.

Tattoo: The bear claw tattoo acts as a talisman to align him with Bear's qualities and powers.

Orca whales: The black and white beasts symbolize yin and yang, the balance and duality of life. Here the orcas, who are mysterious, beautiful, and a bit dangerous, appear as the paddler's allies. In indigenous Pacific Northwestern myths, they are often seen as guardians of the sea and as humanity's helpers.

Salmon: Courage, wisdom, foresight, virility. Pilgrimage and coming home again. The cycle of descent and return.

JOURNAL QUESTIONS

What goal do I need to focus on?

What path am I on?

Where or how do I need to exercise self-discipline in my life?

How can I move forward with confidence?

Am I making progress on my journey?

What does success mean to me?

What will come of testing myself?

How am I being initiated, and into what?

What rite of passage does this initiation signify?

When or how in my life do I feel victorious or triumphant?

What or who is helping me on my journey?

Have I found my place in the world, or am I still seeking it?

What kind of healing does the Canoe offer me?

What kind of healing can I offer the earth
  through the example of the Canoe?

AFFIRMATION

By focusing on my goal, success is mine.

8 · Strength

Courage and Inner Fire

A strong and beautiful woman holds a cougar in her arms. Both wear crowns of flowers. The mountain lion symbolizes her passion, her instincts, her sexuality, and her wildness. Instead of believing her animal nature needs to be subdued, she embraces it and makes it a friend.

Choices are made from the heart. One becomes a bit wilder, more passionate, more creative. The mindful person becomes more spontaneous. There is union between the animal instinctual nature and the "civilized" mind. The infinity sign above her head symbolizes the exchange of energy and information between the left and right sides of the brain—linear and holistic. Inner strength arises naturally from the self-confidence of a balanced, integrated person.

On the rock we see a carving from Italy (500 BCE) that shows a Gorgon Medusa giving birth, assisted by two lionesses. When we call upon on our inner strength, we may be calm and resolute or wild and fierce. Sometimes we are the lady and sometimes the lioness.

When you get this card in a reading ...

You are learning to embrace the wilder, more instinctual facets of your personality. If you were taught to think of the body and the material world as inferior to the mind and spirit, you are now discovering that such is not the case. You are learning to reconsecrate your relationship with your body and with Mother Earth herself.

You may be facing adversity in your life. The development of your inner fortitude is the unseen blessing of difficult times. When you face your fears, when you accept the reality of an unpleasant situation, when you acknowledge the truth you've been avoiding, you develop the courage that allows you to persevere.

If you've never before been tested, you may be surprised to discover a wild source of strength you didn't know you had—like a woman giving birth alone in the wilderness. Afterwards, you are changed, and your sense of personal power grows. Others see it in you and call it "charisma." Your inner fire has been awakened, and it will never again go out.

When you read the Shadow side of this card ...

Be alert that fears and anxieties do not take over a situation. Someone may be denying or repressing their physical or instinctual nature, preferring a life of the mind. When intellect and body are not in harmony, passions and instincts can seem frightening. In this way, there is a chance that someone could be out of control, or using anger and rage in an attempt to dominate. If you are afraid that the difficulties you face are insurmountable, remember that you have deep reserves you have not yet discovered.

Deepen Your Understanding of Strength

THEMES
- Balance of reason and instinct
- Courage, inner fortitude, stamina
- Self-discipline, control, perseverance
- Vitality, joy of life, chi energy or life-force
- Embracing your instinctual, impulsive nature; your inner wild woman or man
- Developing self-confidence by discovering the power within
- Having respect for your inner passions, including your anger
- Defeating an adversary—and better yet: making a friend of a former adversary
- The power to turn an adversary into a friend
- The solar female, in contrast to the Hermit as the lunar male
- Passion, sexuality

SYMBOLS

Lemniscate (infinity sign): Never-ending flow between heaven and earth, spirit and matter, animal and human, instinct and logic. A link to the Magician card.

Sun: Warmth, radiance, brilliance, consciousness, yang.

Woman: The mind, or civilized self, who has integrated the lion's instinctual self.

Lion (Cougar): The instinctual self. Physical strength, vitality, passion. Can represent danger, strong emotions, wildness.

Head wreaths of flowers: Creativity, abundance, beauty, sexuality.

Roses: Passion, love, intoxication.

Rock carving: Gorgon Medusa giving birth, assisted by two lionesses. Inner strength arises inside us when we most need it.

Journal Questions

*What life circumstances have led me to
develop my inner strength?*

How am I "taming the beast" in my life?

How am I expressing my inner wildness?

How do I balance my instincts with my reason?

Have I made a friend of my animal instincts?

What am I passionate about?

Where do I find my lust for life?

How does joy make me strong?

What kind of healing does Strength offer me?

*What kind of healing can I offer the earth
through the example of Strength?*

Affirmation

I face adversity with peaceful courage and inner fire.

9 · The Hermit

Sacred Solitude

The Hermit retreats from the company of others to replenish his soul in solitude as he communes with the natural world. He listens to the calls of birds as he writes and sketches in his journal at twilight time. He ponders his own mortality, and the gifts and challenges of aging. His guardian is the Barred Owl, who sees keenly in the darkness and embodies silent wisdom. From the sacred smoke of burning sage, visions rise of spirit animals. Loon, with an primal eerie call, leads the Hermit into the waters of his dreams and ancestral memories. Wolf, the moon's ally, reminds the Hermit that he is part of a pack or tribe, even when he spends time apart from it. The Merlin is a magical, shapeshifting raptor who shares its name with the wise old man of Arthurian legend. All three are teachers of the Hermit's soul.

When you get this card in a reading...
Your spirit is crying out for a time of sacred solitude. You need to withdraw from the world to focus on your inner

life and spirituality. Perhaps you have been wounded in the "wars of the world," or perhaps you are fatigued and empty from putting out so much energy, especially if you are a caregiver. Your well is empty and needs refilling.

Take some time out for a retreat. Go away to the mountains or the sea, by yourself, without partner or friends. Spend time outside in nature, observing the changes in your environment day by day. Your inner wisdom and sense of well-being will grow effortlessly the more time you spend outside. When you once again enter community life, others will be drawn to the light they see inside you and may come to you for guidance, for part of your purpose is to share what you've learned with others.

When you read the Shadow side of this card...
Some people are afraid of being alone, fearing what they might do or not do if left to themselves. Without some solitude, however, we have difficulty connecting to our authenticity. On the other hand, too much isolation and reclusiveness can lead to loneliness or unhappiness. There may be an opportunity for a personal retreat, but it might seem unaffordable or overindulgent. Instead, find a way to make it happen, because it is necessary for your spiritual health.

Deepen Your Understanding of the Hermit

THEMES

- Solitude
- Withdrawal
- Silence
- Wisdom and experience of age
- The lunar male, in contrast to Strength as the solar female
- Retreat
- Introspection
- Replenishment
- Guiding light
- Communion with the natural world

SYMBOLS

Mountains: Spiritual ascent, clear uncluttered mind, high ideals, peak experience, meeting place of heaven and earth.

Tree: The Tree of Life appears in cross-cultural mythology as a symbol of fertility or everlasting life. In science, it is a metaphor for the evolutionary interrelatedness of living things. In the Kabbalah, it is a diagram of the creation of the world. The World Tree is another cross-cultural symbol that depicts a tree connecting the heavens, the earth, and, with its roots, the underground.

Cloak and hood: Ceremonial clothing of an initiate or academic; the wearer becomes imbued with the power and authority of the subjects he has mastered. Also a reference to archetypal wizards like Merlin and Gandalf.

Burning sage, smoke: Purification, cleansing, creating sacred space.

Lantern: Light of wisdom and knowledge.

Journal and pen: Reflection, introspection, knowledge, learning, wisdom.

Owl: Strength in silence (noiseless flight), night vision, guidance, wisdom.

Wolf: Wolves are often feared by humans but their reputation is not deserved. The concept of a "lone wolf" is a popular one, yet these creatures are highly social and deeply bonded to family and pack. They are known for their loyalty, cunning, intelligence, wisdom, and playfulness. They teach us to howl at the full moon.

Loon: Known for its haunting, eerie call that stirs the wild within us. Can represent solitude, the wilderness, hopes and dreams, lucid dreaming.

Merlin (falcon): A predator who is quick, precise, and graceful, sharing a name with King Arthur's counselor. Brings the gift of making swift, discriminating choices.

JOURNAL QUESTIONS

When was the last time (if ever) I spent a full day and night alone?

How can I get away from everyday life to spend time alone?

Where can I go on retreat?

What are the elements of a great retreat?

How do I feel about being alone?

What are the riches I find in solitude?

How do I feel about the aging process?

What lessons do the spirit animals have for me?

Am I ready to return to the world to share
my light and knowledge?

What kind of healing does the Hermit offer me?

What kind of healing can I offer the earth
through the example of the Hermit?

AFFIRMATION

I retreat from the world in order to refresh my spirit.

10 · The Wheel
(Wheel of Fortune)

Cycles and Seasons

The Wheel of the Year turns and spins, as one season transforms into the next. In this card, the fiery core of the earth is at the still point of the turning world. Trees of each season are rooted in her body. Around the trees we see the eight phases of the moon, which correspond to the eight holy days of the solar year. The zodiac is aligned with the seasons and the lunar phases. For example, the dark/new moon corresponds to winter solstice, the shortest night of the year when the sun begins to wax again. Winter solstice occurs when the sun moves into the sign of Capricorn. So these three—dark/new moon, winter tree, and sign of Capricorn—all line up on the card, and so on around the wheel.

The cycles of nature teach us that all of life moves in a wheel. Wherever we stand on this wheel, we are certain to move to the next point and the one after that, until we are brought full circle to the place where we started, and as T. S. Eliot wrote, we "know the place for the first time."

Outside the wheel of the solar year, the lunar month, and the wheel of the zodiac, we see a circle of prayer beads. This rosary, or mala, is divided into six sets of nine (the magical number of three times three). As we say or sing repetitive prayers, counting beads as we go, we enter an altered state where anything is possible, magic happens, and butterflies—symbol of the soul—break free of the turning of the wheel.

When you get this card in a reading...
You know that change is imminent. One part of a cycle is becoming another. What is passing away in your life right now, and what is coming into being? Where do you stand right now on the wheel? Can you see that what is happening does not happen in isolation, but is part of a pattern?

Sometimes the change that is coming is obvious and striking. More often, it creeps up on us—the trees are suddenly bare and we didn't even notice when the first leaves began to fall. So this card also challenges us to be mindful. Keep track of the sun and moon's cycles, which mirror our own inner cycles.

If things seem chaotic and disorderly in your life, center yourself on the still point of the turning wheel. Constant change is the nature of all that is. When you are centered, you will find that you can trust the turning cycles of change.

When you read the Shadow side of this card ...
There may be an unexpected turn of events. There may
be recurring problems and setbacks; things may seem
to be stagnating. What may feel like bad luck is really
the waning part of a cycle. "What goes up must come
down" is true both of gravity and of the Wheel of Life.

Deepen Your Understanding of the Wheel

THEMES

- Cycles
- Orderly change
- Living in the now
- Turning point
- Seasons, lunar cycles, wheel of the year
- Everything changes
- Impermanence
- Movement

SYMBOLS

Tree: The Tree of Life appears in cross-cultural mythology as a symbol of fertility or everlasting life. In science, it is a metaphor for the evolutionary interrelatedness of living things. In the Kabbalah, it is a diagram of the creation of the world. The World Tree is another cross-cultural symbol that depicts a tree connecting the heavens, earth, and, with its roots, the underground.

Seasons: A result of the tilt of the Earth's axis as the earth revolves around the sun every year. A solar cycle is yang, male, outer-directed.

Lunar phases: A result of the moon's relationship to the sun and its orbit around the Earth every 29.5 days. A lunar cycle is yin, female, inner-directed. The cycle of descent and return.

Zodiac: A ring of constellations in the middle of the ecliptic, or sun's path. The moon and planets also lie within the ecliptic and move through the constellations.

Fire (at earth's core): Transformation, warmth, energy, power, inspiration. Symbolically related to the sun.

Stars: Hope, inspiration, beauty, opportunities, connection with the infinite.

Butterflies: Lightness, joy, transformation, metamorphosis, symbol of the soul.

Prayer beads: The chanting of mantras or prayers. The commitment to a spiritual practice. Connection with all others who pray or meditate.

JOURNAL QUESTIONS

What is changing in my life?

How am I responding to that change?

Am I resisting change and clinging to what is familiar?

In my current project, relationship, or other life cycle—what phase am I in?

How do I stay centered in the midst of change?

Do I have a spiritual practice that helps me navigate the turning of the wheel?

What are my beliefs around destiny and fate?

What can I control in my present situation, and what is beyond my control?

What kind of healing does the Wheel offer me?

What kind of healing can I offer the earth
  through the example of the Wheel?

AFFIRMATION

In centering myself, I am blessed by the turning of the wheel.

11 · Justice

Karmic Balance

Instead of the familiar "scales of justice," we see a
numinous figure who, with his outstretched hands, has
become transformed into the scales himself. He stands
tall and upright, with a look of deep compassion in his
eyes. In one hand he holds a passionate, flaming heart;
in the other, a feather. In Egyptian mythology, the heart
of a person who has recently died is weighed against
the feather of Ma'at, Goddess of Justice. If the scales
balance, he or she is welcomed into Paradise. If the
scales do not balance, the person's heart is devoured by
a demon. The story of Ma'at reminds us that beyond
the social laws of societies and nations is the universal
law of cause and effect, or karmic balance.

Every day we make ethical or unethical choices
that make our hearts lighter or heavier. This happens
on a global level, too. When human beings take what
they want from the natural world without consider-
ing the consequences, devastation occurs. All the plants
and animals pictured on this card are an endangered or
threatened species: spotted owl, American ginseng,

Canada lynx, echinacea, Vancouver Island marmot, Fender's blue butterfly, hawksbill sea turtle, black necked stilt, northern sea otter, trillium, red wolf, and whooping crane. We also see in the distance, a forest of stumps left over from a clearcut. Each of these species has its own story of why it is threatened, and how it might survive. The beauty, mystery, and diversity of our extraordinary planet is diminished every time another species becomes extinct.

The river in the background refers to the many folk songs and hymns that quote Amos 5:24: "Let justice flow like a river and righteousness [right action] like an ever-flowing stream."

Justice asks us to consider the consequences of our actions with each choice we make.

When you get this card in a reading ...
This is a card of cause and effect, of karmic balance. It is time to face the consequences of your past actions, positive or negative. Examine your motives and the values by which you live. Have you acted with unfailing integrity?

Perhaps a conflict is about to be resolved in your life, or a legal matter brought to closure. It may be time for some wrong to be put to right. You find new ways of understanding your place in the web of life, and discover how far-reaching the consequences of your actions can be. It may be time to take a stand for social or environmental justice in your own neighborhood or on a global level. Each of us has a responsibility to leave this world in better shape than we found it.

When you read the Shadow side of this card ...
You are facing an injustice of some kind. This may be on a global or political level, or it may be in your personal life. Someone's rights may have been violated; what can you do to make the situation fair for everyone involved? Also, you may be reaping the outcome of bad habits or unethical choices.

Deepen Your Understanding of Justice

THEMES

- Karma
- Truth
- Social justice
- Responsibility
- Actions and consequences
- Justice
- Right order
- Cause and effect
- Legal issues

SYMBOLS

Man of color: Injustices against minority races or cultures throughout history.

Heart weighed against feather: Represents Ma'at, Egyptian goddess of Justice.

River: Fertility, as the river irrigates land. The never-ending flow of time. Spiritual nourishment.

Endangered species: Injustice. Loving a species to death. Consequences of taking too much.

Clearcut: Same as meaning of endangered species but with trees and plants instead of animals.

JOURNAL QUESTIONS:

Is the current situation about social justice or about my own karma and the consequences of my own actions?

When making a decision or taking action, do I consider the long-term consequences?

Am I tempted to take justice into my own hands when someone has hurt me or to leave justice to the wheels of karma?

If my life were to end tomorrow and my heart was weighed against a feather, would the scales balance?

In what ways do I deflect or defer asking for what is fair to me?

How involved am I in social or environmental causes?

How do I contribute to making the world a better place?

What is the meaning of this quote by Martin Luther King: "The arc of the moral universe is long, but it bends towards justice?"

What kind of healing does Justice offer me?

What kind of healing can I offer the earth through the example of Justice?

AFFIRMATION

I strive to be just and fair in my dealings with others.

12 · The Tree
(The Hanged Man)

Letting Go

The Hanged Man has always been one of the most mysterious and compelling images in the tarot. Here the dreamlike figure is suspended in the yoga posture called *vriksha-asana*—the tree. Her grace and balance mirror the serenity of her inner being. She is able to stay centered even when her world is in upheaval, the horizon is off-kilter, and all things are topsy-turvy.

Perhaps our yogini is right-side up in an upside-down world. Her practice and devotion are evident in the way that she has become one with the sky and sea. She ignores the discomfort of her position, finding harmony with a deeper vision. She shows us how to "let go and let God/dess."

When you get this card in a reading...
It is time to face the truth that the ego's notion of being in control is mostly an illusion. The more we become attuned to Mother Nature, the clearer it becomes that we need times of pause, even reversal, in order to access

a greater wisdom. Although it may be inconvenient or even uncomfortable, allow this flow to move through you. Still your inner noise and surrender to what is.

Your world may feel like it's been turned upside down, or you may feel stuck. Find your center, and don't be afraid. There is an important gift in this—perhaps a new way of seeing, experiencing, or living. Stillness and receptivity are called for. Time spent in suspension clears a space that allows you to experience how the Great Mystery acts for your highest good. By not forcing things, you may receive gifts of enlightenment and experience divine, unconditional love.

When you read the Shadow side of this card...

The ego refuses to surrender, and chooses instead to be mired in an unwinnable situation. Blocks and hang-ups may become increasingly frustrating as lessons are disregarded. What inevitability is being ignored? Who is in denial? If patience is called for, be sure to take as much time as necessary. Haste or aggressiveness may undermine the balance or peace.

Deepen Your Understanding of the Tree

THEMES

- Surrender
- Release
- Suspension
- Reversal
- Letting go of control
- Find a new perspective
- Sacrifice

Symbols

Tree (Bigleaf Maple): The Tree of Life appears in cross-cultural mythology as a symbol of fertility or everlasting life. In science, it is a metaphor for the evolutionary interrelatedness of living things. In the Kabbalah, it is a diagram of the creation of the world. The World Tree is another cross-cultural symbol that depicts a tree connecting the heavens, the earth, and, with its roots, the underground. The indigenous Northwest people called the bigleaf maple the "paddle tree," since they carved paddles, bowls, spoons, and other tools out of its wood. This tree of life also provided them with food and medicine.

Falling leaves and seedpods: Old ideas, beliefs, memories, teachings that have outlived their usefulness. The end of a season or cycle, the need to slow down. Release and letting go.

Chickadee: Can be seen feeding upside-down from tree limbs.

Namaste (placement of hands): The Divine in me bows to the Divine in you.

Vriksha-asana (yoga posture): Regular practice promotes balance, stability, focus, and concentration.

Fluffy white clouds: Positive thinking, thoughts, ideals, hopes, prayers, intentions, affirmations.

Water, mild turbulence: Emotional turmoil, upset.

Tilted horizon line: World is in upheaval from your perspective.

Peaceful facial expression: Serenity, calm, peace of mind.

JOURNAL QUESTIONS

How can I let go?

What do I need to surrender?

How can I look at the present situation from a different perspective?

What discoveries might await me if I venture outside the box of my comfort zone?

What is holding me up?

What is hanging me up?

How might yoga benefit me?

What can I change?

What or who can I not change?

What kind of healing does the Tree offer me?

What kind of healing can I offer the earth through the example of the Tree?

AFFIRMATION

I find serenity in surrendering my life to the Great Mystery.

13 · Death

Dying and Being Born

A heron lies dead in an old decaying boat near the beach. Ants and spiders crawl on the carcass and a vulture hovers overhead. Wild roses and elderberry grow up through the rotting boat and butterflies flit through the greenery. Sinuous ropes like snakes are coiled below the deck. To the west are the islands of the Otherworld, and late afternoon sunlight sparkles on the water.

In Celtic mythology, the Otherworld—often conceived as islands—always lies to the west, and travelers often set off on their last journey by boat. Heron is a guardian spirit who stands at the gateway of life and death. Vultures feed on dead flesh and purify it, leaving only bones behind. Elderberry is an herb that is both medicinal and toxic.

The flash of sunlight on water has been called the "White Lady" in some Celtic traditions, and is seen as an epiphany or manifestation of the Goddess. When the heron sails home through the gates of the Otherworld, those of us who are left behind stand in awe of the Great Mystery.

When you get this card in a reading...

Something in your life is dying, while something else is nearing its time to be born. Take the time that you need to recognize that this is a natural process, a part of the great cycle of all life. Grieve if you need to for that which is ending, whether it is a cherished dream, a relationship, or a belief system. Don't rush the process or deny all your turbulent feelings. Whether a literal death or the ending of a chapter in your life, death isn't pretty and it can hurt. It's painful. Whatever dies is gone, and it will never return again in the same form.

But just as the dark moon gives way to the new and winter gives way to spring, rebirth will surely follow death. Releasing that which no longer serves your best interests clears the space for new beginnings and an upsurge of vitality. When you are ready to let go of grief, you will find yourself emptied out and clean, ready for the next stage of your journey.

When you read the Shadow side of this card...

Profound, permanent loss or change may be triggering intense fears of the unknown. The changes that are occurring may be needed, but there is denial around them, especially if it requires a loss of control or power. Ours is a culture that fears and hides from death, so it would not be surprising for someone to resist the process. Someone may be in deep pain over that which is ending, unable to move past grief. This may be a time of stagnation or procrastination. Beware of a pessimistic or even deeply depressed mindset.

Deepen Your Understanding of Death

THEMES

- Transformation
- Conclusion
- Transition
- Physical death
- Ending
- Renewal

SYMBOLS

Boat: The spiritual body or soul. The transition from the material to the spirit world. A crossing made by the living or the dead. The means by which we reach Paradise, after death. A boat may also be identified with a bodhisattva or saint who embodies safety while the pilgrim travels on the rough seas of life.

Heron: A liminal waterbird who stands motionless at the border of land and water, as if she were a guardian or sentinel. Peace, serenity, grace, independence, self-reflection. Like all birds, a messenger between heaven and earth.

Vulture: One who eats the flesh of the dead, helping the corpse return to the earth. Death and decay.

Islands, especially those in the west: Paradise, the Otherworld. When reached at the end of a long journey, a spiritual center. Sanctuary. The dwelling place of practitioners of healing, peace, and knowledge. The desire for earthly or eternal happiness.

Sunlight sparkling on water: The White Lady, a goddess in Celtic lands.

Water/the sea: Feelings, emotions, the unconscious. Hidden or secret teachings. That which we cross to reach the Otherworld. Primordial soup, from which all life arises. Life/death/rebirth.

Mast and sail: They form a cross, the Christian symbol of resurrection.

Ropes and floats: Similar in shape to snakes and eggs, both symbols of transformation and rebirth.

Elderberry (red): In folklore and poetry, the elder tree has been associated with death and with the land of Faery. The elder tree itself is prolific and will regenerate from any part, even when the gardener has hacked it down to the ground.

Wild roses: Love, rebirth, the soul's perfection. Emblem of Aphrodite/Venus and Mary, symbols of divine womanhood. The five petaled rose is related to the pentacle, a symbol of the four elements plus the element of spirit.

Rose thorns: The pain that sometimes comes along with love and passion.

Butterflies: Lightness, joy, transformation, metamorphosis, the soul.

Journal Questions

What is ending, or needs to end, in my life?

How might this ending be a blessing in disguise?

In what way might pruning back the dead wood or unnecessary in my life bring about a new vitality?

What are my beliefs about death?

Am I prepared for my own death?

Do I have a will and other necessary end-of-life documents in place?

What kind of end-of-life care do I want to have?

What do I want done with my remains after I die?

How do I honor that which has ended in my life?

How do I remember my beloved dead?

What kind of healing does Death offer me?

What kind of healing can I offer the earth through the example of Death?

Affirmation

I accept the change that Death brings in order that I may receive the transformation of rebirth.

14 · Temperance

Combining Opposites

The winged one lifts a shell to pour out her blessings into a bowl of burning herbs. Instead of water, she pours the refracted light of a rainbow. Her third eye glows with sacred knowledge and far-sight. The steam-filled pool distorts her reflection—or is the distortion an accurate picture of another kind? She is a mixed-race child; the bloodlines of many cultures run within her body. By her example, she calls to us to integrate all the disparate parts of ourselves. Her gifts are those of healing, creativity, and the integration of light and shadow within us.

The word temperance comes from the Latin *temperare*, "to combine" or "to mix." This card is about combining diverse elements to create something new. As such, it is often the signature card of artists. Blue and red make purple; rain and sun make rainbows; water and fire make steam. The full moon rises as the sun sets; the sun rises as the full moon sets. This perfect balance of opposites graces us with extraordinary beauty.

When you get this card in a reading...
Temperance offers the serenity of the middle way between polarities. Embrace the different parts of your personality and life's experiences, both light and shadow, joyful and painful. They all combine together, resulting in your unique individuality. This is an opportunity for the inner, spiritual life to harmonize with the external life of the workaday world. Temperance offers the discovery that your whole life is a work of art. It also indicates someone who may be in need of healing on a spiritual or physical level, and the Winged One—a descendant of the ancient bird goddesses—will facilitate that. She may also guide you into the role of becoming a healer yourself.

When you read the Shadow side of this card...
There could be difficulty finding a balancing point between two polarities or sides of an issue, with one side or the other being more weighed down. If someone is taking an extreme stance, and refusing to consider moderation or cooperation, encourage them to take the middle road. There may be a struggle to harmonize or blend different elements, conflicts, or opposing sides. Perhaps situations are being made worse due to a failure to come to terms with difficulty, loss, or other shadow issues. Integration and healing are needed.

Deepen Your Understanding of Temperance

THEMES

- Balancing opposites
- Art and creativity
- Seeking resolution
- Finding a third (middle) way
- Owning your own light and shadow
- Blending opposites to create something new

- Moderation
- Healing
- Tempering

SYMBOLS

Angel or bird goddess: The earliest images of bird goddesses are found in Neolithic Europe and predate the concept of angels. The Christian iconography of angels seems to be directly derived from Egyptian and Hellenistic winged goddesses and gods beginning around 500 BCE. Whether angel or bird goddess, the image of a woman with wings indicates an ability to "fly" or cross easily between the worlds of spirit and matter.

Mixed race woman: The blending of cultures and bloodlines creates richness and beauty.

Rainbow: Beauty, hope, a range of possibilities, harmonious blending of colors.

Sunset/sunrise: Beautiful, liminal times of transformation.

Shell: The element of water: emotions, dreams, fantasies, spirituality.

Burning herbs: The element of fire: passion, creativity, energy, power.

Steaming pool: Combination of water and fire (heat).

Iris: Emblem of the Greek rainbow goddess, a messenger of the gods (inner guides). She traveled the rainbow bridge between the worlds.

JOURNAL QUESTIONS

How can I balance opposites?

How can I find the middle way?

What can I create that is new and unique from two polarities?

What am I tempering?

How am I an artist?

How am I a healer?

Have I integrated the light and shadow sides of my personality?

What setbacks or losses in my life have opened the doorway to unexpected blessings?

What kind of healing does Temperance offer me?

What kind of healing can I offer the earth through the example of Temperance?

AFFIRMATION

I combine and blend opposites to create something beautiful and unique.

15 · Bindweed
(The Devil)

Life Out of Balance

The previous card, Temperance, reminds us to live a balanced life. The Bindweed card depicts a life lived desperately out of balance. The figure is in despair, bound to his own addictions. He sees no way out. His internal struggle is reflected in the world around him, where non-native invasive plants and birds crowd out native species, causing a severe imbalance in the ecosystem.

Although bindweed flowers (of the morning glory family) look lovely and pristine white, the plant runs rampant, curling itself around the stems and branches of healthy plants until they wither away for lack of sunlight.

In the sky behind the figure, a flock of starlings (a non-native species in North America) swoops by, decimating the habitat of native birds. More starlings chatter with each other above the figure, like voices in his head that won't go away. Will the figure break free of his bonds? Will he find his way back to health and harmony? Perhaps he will need to pull the bindweed up by

the roots and burn it before he can bring his life back
into balance.

When you get this card in a reading...
Ask yourself: what holds you in bondage? What in
your life, or around you, takes more than its fair share
of attention, energy, and life force? What are the roots
of despair? What lies are being told and believed? Bindweed warns that someone is playing power games,
resulting in domination and control. Awareness is
needed. Ignorance leads to fear of the unknown; the
inability to love leads to isolation and depression. When
addictions—whether they be drugs, alcohol, sugar,
shopping, TV, or any other "drug" of choice—run
loose in our lives, they create chaos. Immediate action
is called for in order to restore balance.

When you read the Shadow side of this card...
This is either a situation in which addictions and denial
are becoming even more deeply entrenched, or else
(more likely) you are breaking free of them. If so, celebrate and give thanks for the breakthrough that has
broken the bonds. Whoever has been in emotional,
spiritual, or habitual slavery is now free. The fears
that created inaction and self-sabotage no longer have
power. Commit to being vigilant and proactive so this
painful lesson does not recur.

Deepen Your Understanding of Bindweed

THEMES

- Life out of balance
- Free yourself
- Ignorance
- Bondage
- Oppression
- Materialism
- Addictions
- Despair
- Limitations

SYMBOLS

Man's posture: Despair, depression, closed to outside intervention. Negative emotions locked into the body.

Bindweed (morning glories): A lovely yet invasive plant that runs rampant. It strangles other plants and is nearly impossible to eradicate.

Starlings: An invasive species that proliferates in North America, crowding out native species.

Dead shrub: The life has been choked out of it by the bindweed that covers it.

JOURNAL QUESTIONS

What holds me in bondage?

What is out of balance in my life?

What consumes too much of my time and attention?

What are my own Shadow aspects that I deny or fail to acknowledge?

When have I been less than truthful to myself or others?

Who or what do I tend to give my power away to? Why?

How can I free myself of that which holds me in bondage?

What kind of healing does Bindweed offer me?

What kind of healing can I offer the earth
   through the example of Bindweed?

AFFIRMATION

I bring my life back into balance by breaking free of the fears that keep me trapped.

16 · Lightning
(The Tower)

Sudden, Irrevocable Change

Lightning strikes a tree and lights it on fire as a thunderstorm rages. Three figures fall out of the sky, as if in a dream. When lightning strikes, there is an increase of ozone and oxidants in the atmosphere, which cleanses the air. In the same way, the aftermath of a calamity can bring about renewal in our lives.

In Celtic folklore, it is said that a tree which survives a lightning bolt often flourishes afterwards. People take pieces of such trees to bless their homes and draw good luck. In some indigenous cultures, a person who survives being struck by lightning may become a shaman and healer.

This card is one of sudden, irrevocable change unlike the Wheel, where change occurs in cycles and patterns. Lightning's change can be as catastrophic as an earthquake or terrorist attack, or as illuminating as a sudden flash of insight. In either case, life will never be the same.

When you get this card in a reading…

Get ready, because life as you have known it may be in for a sudden, radical change. It may be an epiphany or a flash of insight that totally revises the way you look at the world. It may be an emotional breakthrough. Or it may be an upheaval in your life or in the world around you. Something taken for granted—whether good or ill—is teetering on a precipice.

If you resist breaking free of bondage, as the Bindweed card encourages us to do, you may be setting yourself up for a Lightning experience. If you can't bring yourself to make necessary changes, it may be taken out of your hands with a cataclysmic external experience or by cosmic intervention.

What kinds of sweeping revisions, letting go, and clearing are needed? Who or what is the catalyst of this revolutionary moment? The strike of the lightning bolt can both destroy and transform. It can illuminate while also burning away that which will not survive. The energy released in the aftermath of this crisis has the potential for enormous creativity and transformation.

When you read the Shadow side of this card…

The upheaval is probably a smaller one, and not as radical or life-changing. Fears and avoidance may be postponing a needed change or upheaval. The situation may be lasting longer than had been expected. Beware of allowing these changes to create bitterness and despair. Attempting to control outcomes may not be productive. Instead, use this as an opportunity to deepen your courage, accepting that there is usually an important gift hidden in the rubble of what has fallen. You may be ready to begin the healing process.

Deepen Your Understanding of Lightning

THEMES

- Shocking events
- Dramatic change
- Epiphany
- Disruption
- Chaos
- Sudden upheaval
- Revelation
- Crisis
- Burst of insight

SYMBOLS

Lightning bolt: Sudden revelation. Intuitive flashes and illumination. Being struck by lightning is said to awaken latent psychic powers. Also, divine justice and the power to change things quickly. "Fire from heaven" which is either life-giving or death-dealing. Sky gods like Thor and Zeus throw lightning bolts to demonstrate power and might.

Stormy, red sky: Omen of disaster. A red sky in the morning is a harbinger of an oncoming storm.

Falling: A fall from grace, plans falling through, heading for a fall, falling in love, falling down on the job, taking the blame as the fall guy. A precarious position, feeling insecure and vulnerable. Out of control.

Tree: The Tree of Life appears in cross-cultural mythology as a symbol of fertility or everlasting life. In science, it is a metaphor for the evolutionary inter-relatedness of living things. In the Kabbalah, it is a diagram of the creation of the world. The World Tree is another cross-cultural symbol that depicts a tree connecting the heavens, the earth, and, with its roots, the underground.

Journal Questions

What sudden revelation have I recently had?

How is my life radically changing?

What attitudes need to be banished in order for me to move on?

What insights reveal new possibilities to me?

What limiting circumstances am I released from?

What is true security and false security in my life?

When I've lost everything, what remains?

What kind of healing does Lightning offer me?

What kind of healing can I offer the earth through the example of Lightning?

Affirmation

I am transformed and liberated by my acceptance of profound change.

17 · The Star

Opening to Grace

A time of peace and tranquility follows the lightning and storms of the previous card. A woman kneels before a sacred spring filled with starlight. In her hands, she cups the water of life. Soon she will take a deep drink and be filled with renewal, hope, and inspiration. Her body becomes suffused with light as she experiences herself as one with all beings.

Above her, the Pleaides rise, those dancing seven sisters who symbolize our heart's home. Behind her is the celestial stream between heaven and earth, known as the Milky Way, where pilgrims travel from one realm to the next. Beside her, the Kingfisher reminds us of the halcyon days of peace and plenty. With our inner ear, we hear a voice proclaim: "I am the Soul of Nature, which gives Life to the Universe. From me all things proceed, and to me all things shall return." More than anything, the Star Goddess represents grace, a divine connection that is unearned and freely granted.

Let us take our hope and inspiration from the star of wonder. May she remind us to offer up a prayer of thanksgiving for the multitude of blessings in our lives.

When you get this card in a reading...

You have the opportunity to relax into a time of calm, healing and grace. Your heart is wide open and you deeply feel your connection to Source, God/dess, and the Great Mystery. It is a most blessed time of hope, peace, and well-being. You may experience yourself as part of a cosmic pattern, connected to everything in the universe. This experience has been called nirvana, enlightenment, awakening. Cherish this experience when it is time for you to come back to everyday life. "Before enlightenment, chop wood, carry water," goes the Zen saying. "After enlightenment, chop wood, carry water." Your cosmic experience has made all the difference, and your daily tasks are now suffused with the Divine's presence.

Now is a good time to begin the practice of gratitude, of giving thanks. When our hearts are full, it's easy to be thankful. If we begin the practice now, it will be easier to sustain when times are rough. Follow your star—it will guide you home.

When you read the Shadow side of this card...

You may be feeling hopeless and unable to connect with Spirit. Healing may be taking longer than you had expected. Doubt or insecurity may be blocking the Star's promise. What is causing the blockage and what can you do to remove it? You may be experiencing a "dark night of the soul," as if you are descending to the Underworld like Persephone or Inanna. Remember that when each returned at last to the world of the living, they became the queens of both realms.

Deepen Your Understanding of the Star

THEMES

- Hope
- Wonder
- Serenity
- Refreshment
- Gratitude
- Grace
- Mystical experience
- Peace
- Spiritual blessing
- Inspiration
- Generosity

SYMBOLS

Starry sky: Hope, inspiration, beauty, opportunities, connection with the infinite.

Milky Way: A pathway that links the Earth to the Otherworld in most cultures around the world. Souls, birds, pilgrims, and mystics travel on it between the worlds. In other stories, it may represent a serpent, a seam, a felled tree, a celestial stream, the chain of the Celtic god Lugh, the breast milk of the Greek goddess Hera, or the nourishing milk of the Egyptian cow goddess Hathor. It marks the boundary between busy earthly concerns and the still silence of the universe.

Pleiades: A small cluster of stars, of which seven are the brightest, found in the Taurus constellation. They are a prominent and much-loved sight in the Northern Hemisphere in winter and the Summer Hemisphere in summer. Their rising signals the change of seasons. The brightest of the seven stars is the Greek *Alcyone* (Halcyon), whose name means peace. In cross-cultural mythology, they've been known as seven sisters, seven doves or water birds, the Fates, or the prow of a canoe paddled across the sky. They are also a symbol for one's ancestral home; many indigenous people in Australia as well as North America have origin stories that say their particular tribe descends from the Pleiades.

Spring: The source of spiritual refreshment, healing, prosperity.

Ferns, moss: The life-force in plants.

White gown: Purity, cleanliness.

Kingfisher: A legendary bird, usually identified with the kingfisher, symbolizes the "halcyon days," a time of peace and plenty. In Greek mythology, this referred to the week before and the week after the Winter Solstice. According to legend, the sea was completely calm during this time, while the halcyon bird built her nest upon the waves and hatched her chicks.

Sphere of light: Wholeness, inspiration, hope, promise, magic.

Journal Questions

What gives me hope?

What kind of spiritual practice do I have?

How do I connect with the Great Mystery, God/dess?

What inspires me?

When have I experienced complete well-being, peace and joy?

How can I experience it again?

How can I bring peace into my world?

What is the North Star or guiding light of my life?

Where is my heart's home?

What kind of healing does the Star offer me?

*What kind of healing can I offer the earth
through the example of the Star?*

Affirmation

I open up to the peace and inspiration of the Great
Mystery.

18 · The Moon

Constant, Faithful Changes

La Luna Bella! A woman invokes the energies of the full moon, while all around her spiral the eight lunar phases. Each month the moon embodies the cycle of descent and return, as it waxes to fullness, wanes to darkness, and begins to wax again. The Moon is constantly changing, and is utterly faithful in her changes.

This cycle embodies one of the most profound teachings that Nature has to offer us. Every month the lunar cycle, which is mirrored in a woman's menstrual cycle, reminds us that one stage of life always succeeds another, and that times of darkness are always followed by renewal.

Behind the woman we see the paleolithic relief of the Great Goddess of Laussel, which may be humankind's first calendar. With one hand she points to her belly (hidden behind the woman's head) and with the other, holds aloft a crescent-shaped horn incised with thirteen notches, the number of lunations in a solar year. The woman is accompanied by those allies of the night, Owl and Wolf. Owl teaches us to navigate using our feelings, instinct, and intuition. Wolf teaches us to get in touch with our "wildish" nature and howl at the luminous moon. Salmon leaps up from the depths, bringing the wisdom of its own cycle of descent and return.

When you get this card in a reading …
It is time to raise your lunar consciousness. Begin to track the movement of the moon in the night sky where you live. Where does it rise and where does it set? And at what times of day and night? Which phase is it in tonight?

As you look at the Moon card, which lunar phase draws your eye? Which phase relates to a current situation? Perhaps this is a new relationship, or time to leave a job. The lunar cycle is a model for any life cycle, whether it is a relationship, a job, or a creative project. Knowing your place in this cycle can help put your current issues in perspective.

In addition, this card indicates an awakening of powerful psychic abilities and learning to trust one's intuition. This may be frightening or confusing for those who have depended only on guidance of the clear light of rationality. The more familiar we become with the language of dreams, symbol and myth, the more comfortable we can be with the gifts the Moon has to offer. Keep a dream journal, study the arts of divination and magic, learn to trust your intuition.

When you read the Shadow side of this card ...
This is the terrain of nightmares, phobias, anxieties, and illusions. Someone is resisting the idea of opening up to the psychic, non-rational realms. A difficult emotional journey may be at hand. This may feel like a journey into darkness, and may trigger a confrontation with your deepest fears. Remember that sometimes what we fear in the darkness may be revealed as harmless in the light of day. Ask for a reality check from trusted loved ones if you need to. Embrace your own Shadow, for it is only when we love the most unlovable parts of ourselves that we can truly heal.

THEMES

- Constant, faithful changes
- Cycle of descent and return
- Psychic awakening
- Light and shadow
- Intuition
- Dreams
- Imagination

SYMBOLS

Lunar phases: A result of the moon's relationship to the sun and its orbit around the Earth every 29.5 days. A lunar cycle is yin, female, inner-directed. The cycle of descent and return.

Great Goddess of Laussel: Carved some 20,000 years ago above the entrance to a cave in France. Archeologists speculate that this image represents the first calendar, created by women who noticed the correlation between their bleeding cycles and the cycle of the moon, which both last approximately 29 days.

Salmon: Wisdom, knowledge, second sight, poetic inspiration (Celtic). Spiritual nourishment, determination, renewal (Northwest Native American).

Owl: Strength in silence (noiseless flight), night vision, guidance, wisdom. Can also symbolize death and ghosts.

Wolf: Wolves are often feared by humans but their reputation is not deserved. They are often depicted as the solitary "lone wolf," yet they are highly social and deeply bonded to family and pack. They are known for their loyalty, cunning, intelligence, wisdom and playfulness. And they teach us to howl at the full moon.

Water/the sea: Feelings, emotions, the unconscious. Hidden or secret teachings. That which we cross to reach the Otherworld. Primordial soup, from which all life arises. Life/death/rebirth.

Whirlpool: Pulls us "down the drain," into a descent to the unconscious, the place where dreams, symbol, myth and shadows rule.

Islands: Paradise, the Otherworld. When reached at the end of a long journey, a spiritual center. Sanctuary. The dwelling place of practitioners of healing, peace and knowledge. The desire for earthly or eternal happiness.

Journal Questions

How can I become more moon-wise?

Am I aware of what phase the Moon is in right now, without looking it up in a book or online?

Do I know where the Moon rises and sets on the horizon near my home, and at what time?

Which phase of the Moon do I most identify with, right now?

Do I consider myself to be psychic or intuitive?

Am I scared by the idea of receiving information from a "sixth sense?"

Do I pay attention to my dreams?

What kind of healing does the Moon offer me?

What kind of healing can I offer the earth through the example of the Moon?

Affirmation

I am in harmony with the waxing and waning of my emotions and intuition.

19 · The Sun

Radiant Joy

From the shadows of the Moon, we move into the clear light of day. A woman dances for joy at the peak of the sun's power, at noon on the summer solstice. Even the sunflowers behind her are radiating happiness. As she dances, she experiences that sensation known as "flow." She is so focused and engaged in her dancing that she loses all sense of self and of the passage of time. She has learned how to create happiness for herself by living a life of purpose and by sharing her joy with others. There is no hidden agenda here, no sadness or darkness or stress, just the sheer joy of being alive.

When you get this card in a reading...
You may find a big smile on your face. With a huge burst of energy, your spirit is shouting out a great big YES! You are healthy, energetic, and enthusiastic, with a warm and generous heart. It is your time to shine in the world. Perhaps you have accomplished a long term goal or are receiving accolades and attention for the good work you have done. Perhaps you have begun to

notice the small moments, every day, that make you happy. On some level, you have chosen to be happy and have created a life that supports it. Now is the time to engage with family, friends, and community. Step into the flow of creativity or other favorite activities where worry and self-consciousness cease to exist. When our hearts are open, it is easy and a great pleasure to share and be of service. Celebrate and get out and play in the sunshine. Sing, dance, make love, let your creativity run free. Shine on!

When you read the Shadow side of this card...
You may find that your overall happiness and satisfaction is lessened a bit, and you may need to take some action towards creating more joy in your life. On the other hand, life may be too intense and you may be experiencing burnout. There may be a hidden agenda, or something that had seemed simple and straightforward is more problematic than first thought. Again, time to make some changes. What steps can you take each day to maintain a high level of satisfaction and joy?

Deepen Your Understanding of the Sun

THEMES

- Happiness
- Consciousness
- Good health
- Radiance
- Illumination
- Out in the open; nothing is hidden
- Being the center of attention

- Joy
- Vitality
- Celebration
- Enthusiasm

SYMBOLS

Sun: Warmth, radiance, brilliance, clarity, vitality, joy. Yang in contrast to the Moon's yin.

Sunflowers: Faithfulness and constancy. They follow the sun's path through the sky, as people are drawn to those who radiate happiness.

Red (dress and scarf): Vitality, passion, love, energy.

Stone wall: Keeping your boundaries strong so that you stay away from the mindset and habits that bring unhappiness.

Yellow (flowers): Mimicking the happiness of the sun.

Green grass: The vitality of all growing things.

Noon: The peak of the sun's power during the day.

Journal Questions

Where do I find happiness?

How do I create happiness in my life?

When do I experience "flow"?

What am I celebrating?

How have I achieved success?

What brings me joy?

How do I share my happiness with others?

What is now completely clear?

What kind of healing does the Sun offer me?

What kind of healing can I offer the earth
through the example of the Sun?

Affirmation

I choose to make a life that creates happiness for myself
and others.

20 · Awakening (Judgement)

Getting Conscious

With this card, we awaken to a higher level of consciousness, both on the personal and planetary levels. We are called to open our hearts to Spirit, to live in a more meaningful way, and to participate in the life of our communities. We "think globally and act locally" and are aware of the dakinis, angels, and bodhisattvas that aid us behind the scenes as we work to heal the planet.

In this image, a young man opens up to the life of the Spirit. He has emerged from the darkness of the tomb/womb of Newgrange and is now following the spiral path of the devotee. The compassionate gaze of Kwan Yin, goddess of mercy, smiles down upon him. Cranes of peace fly overhead.

His community encircles him, between the earth and the heavens, creating sacred space where all things are possible. Magic happens, the earth is healed, and so are we.

When you get this card in a reading ...

You become aware of a shift in your consciousness. In a way, you have "woken up." Perhaps you have made a commitment to eating locally grown organic foods, or perhaps you've begun a new spiritual practice. You now perceive yourself to be part of the global community. You know that your choices and actions affect the entire web of life, and you live your life accordingly.

As you continue to open yourself up to the life of the Spirit, your heart is filled with compassion and you begin to let go of the judgments and criticisms you have made in the past. To live in alignment with your deepest, most authentic Self is not possible without the help of spiritual allies. This knowledge keeps us humble.

You know your life has purpose and meaning, and this gives you deep joy and peace. Service to others may not have been part of your life in the past, but it is now. When you give your own unique gift to the world, the entire fabric of the planet is strengthened and enriched.

When you read the Shadow side of this card ...

You may be attached to old ways of doing things and are unwilling to hear the call of the Spirit. Even when old beliefs are not truly authentic, or no longer serve the highest good, it may be difficult to let go, if only because they are so familiar. There could be a resistance to guidance, a need for control, or a preference for what is known and comfortable, even if founded on negative habit patterns. Remember, as Anaïs Nin wrote, the day may come "when the risk to remain tight in a bud [is] more painful than the risk it [takes] to blossom."

Deepen your understanding of Awakening

THEMES

- Expanded consciousness
- Personal awakening
- Birth of a new paradigm
- Liberation
- Mindfulness
- Peace
- Mass awakening
- Think globally, act locally
- Awareness
- Rebirth
- Inner calling; what you are meant to do with your life

SYMBOLS

Newgrange: A prehistoric passage tomb in the Boyne River Valley in Ireland. Built approximately 5,000 years ago, it was constructed so that the long passage and central chamber are illuminated by the sun at dawn each winter solstice. It is a potent symbol of death and rebirth.

Spirals (carved on the Newgrange entrance stone): Contraction and expansion, repetitive rhythm of life, cyclical nature of evolution, constant flux and movement, symbol of the soul's journey. Found in every culture.

Circle of people creating sacred space: Unity, magic, community, connection.

Man with arms uplifted: Worship, awe, reverence, opening up to the Spirit.

Cranes: Japanese symbol of honor, loyalty, eternity, and peace. Ten years after the atomic bomb fell on Hiroshima, a young girl died from leukemia caused by radiation from the bomb. Before she died, she folded a thousand origami cranes based on the legend that whoever folded a thousand cranes would be granted a wish. A thousand paper cranes is now a symbol of international peace, especially for children.

Kwan Yin: Goddess of mercy and compassion, much beloved all over the world. She is a "mother of mercy" like Mary and Tara; all three have been called "She Who Hears the Cries of the World."

Lotus: In Hinduism and Buddhism, a symbol of enlightenment, purity, awakening, and the progress of the soul. The perfect lotus rises out of muddy waters to float on the surface and bask in the sunlight, a metaphor for the progress of the soul. It opens in the morning and closes at night, a symbol of death and rebirth.

Candles: Illuminate the darkness; represent prayers, wishes, spells or offerings; create sacred space; hope, enlightenment, the human spirit.

Awakening: "We fulfill our destiny and realize our purpose when we awaken to who we are: conscious Presence."—Eckhart Tolle.

JOURNAL QUESTIONS

What does it mean to be awakened?

How has my consciousness been raised?

What call of the Spirit am I hearing?

How can I release my criticism and judgements of others?

How can I be of service to others?

What unique gift do I have to offer the world?

What kind of healing does Awakening offer me?

What kind of healing can I offer the earth through the example of Awakening?

AFFIRMATION

I awaken to the call of the Spirit.

21 · Gaia, the World

May All Beings Be Blessed

The silver-haired Grandmother of All holds Mother Earth in her arms, gazing at her with all the joy and tenderness a mother has for her newborn child. The Daughter is here too, in the form of a swallowtail butterfly. (Can this be the same swallowtail we saw on the Seeker card?) Prayers for the planet are perpetually made as prayer flags flutter in the breeze. The wreath of blessing herbs—cedar, sage, sweetgrass, and lavender—creates the mandorla gateway, guarded by animals of the four directions. May all beings be blessed. May there be peace on our beloved Mother Gaia.

When you get this card in a reading...
You know that "all shall be well," as the medieval mystic Julian of Norwich sang. This card is the best of all possible cards to get in a reading, because it represents the culmination of your spiritual journey. It signifies wholeness and an integration of your spiritual, emotional and physical lives. A major stage or cycle of your life is complete, and a new one will soon begin. Receiving this card

invites you to pause before the next chapter and celebrate the fullness of this time. Before you rush into becoming the Seeker once more, allow this important completion to fill your heart with gratitude and profound joy. You may have had a transcendent epiphany where you became aware of the life-energy of the planet and experienced Mother Earth as a living being. This kind of cosmic consciousness is hard to describe but once experienced, is always part of you. Your life becomes a cosmic dance in which you forget and remember, forget and remember. When this card appears, you remember your birthright as a child of Heaven and Earth.

When you read the Shadow side of this card...
The full meaning of this card is diminished only a bit. Your current life cycle is not yet complete, or your joy is not quite as full as it otherwise could be. Step outside of your own situation to make prayers for the planet and all her creatures.

Deepen Your Understanding of Gaia, the World

THEMES

- Wholeness
- Success
- Cooperative humanity
- Fulfillment
- Integration
- Unity
- Wellness
- Completion
- Thanksgiving
- Accomplishment

Symbols

Grandmother or Crone: The archetypal wise woman. She passes on her wisdom and teachings to younger generations. She is honored and respected for her life experience.

Tibetan prayer flags: It is believed that the wind carries the prayers and mantras written on the flags all over the world, spreading good will, peace, compassion, and wisdom.

Planet: The planet Earth is 4.6 billion years old! "We have a beautiful mother," Alice Walker writes. "Her green lap immense, her brown embrace eternal, her blue body everything we know."

Halo: In the religious iconography of many cultures, a sacred or holy figure is indicated by a radiant or bright circle around the head and shoulders. Some say it is a depiction of the aura (energy field) that emanates from the being.

Mandorla: An almond-shaped opening or halo, also known as the *vesica piscis* (the space where two circles overlap). In religious iconography, it frames the whole body instead of just the head and shoulders. Its shape is the same as that of the yoni (vulva), the gateway to life.

Butterfly: Lightness, joy, transformation, metamorphosis, symbol of the soul.

Blessing herbs: Used in many cultures to purify and bless people, ceremonial spaces, or tools. The herbs are often burned and the smoke banishes negative energies and attracts positive ones. Essential oils can also be sprayed into the air for similar effect.

Lavender: Purification, cleanliness, calm, peacefulness. From the Latin *lavare*, "to wash."

Sage: Purification, banishing of negative energy or influences. From the Latin *salvare*, "to heal."

Cedar: A most sacred, ancient and wise of all trees to Pacific Northwest indigenous peoples. The smoke carries prayers to the Creator. Like sage, it is used for banishing negative energy and like sweetgrass, it brings in blessings.

Sweetgrass: Healing and blessing. Brings in the good energy after sage and cedar have purified the space of negative energy. In medieval Europe, "holy grass" was strewn on church floors so the sweet vanilla scent would rise as people walked on it.

Eagle: Symbol of the element of air and the direction of east.

Snake: Symbol of the element of fire and the direction of south.

Salmon: Symbol of the element of water and the direction of west.

Deer: Symbol of the element of earth and the direction of north.

Journal Questions

What cycle is reaching completion in my life?

How am I blessed?

*Is my life balanced on spiritual, emotional,
mental, and physical levels?*

*Have I ever had a mystical experience where I
experienced oneness with the universe? What
happened after that experience faded?*

What kind of daily spiritual practice do I have?

What is my relationship with the Earth?

*What do I believe about the universe,
the earth, and god/dess?*

What kind of healing does Gaia, the World, offer me?

*What kind of healing can I offer the earth through
the example of Gaia, the World?*

Affirmation

All shall be well, and all shall be well, and all manner of
things shall be well.

The Minor Arcana:
Elements, Numbers, People

Earth my body
Water my blood
Air my breath, and
Fire my spirit

—Contemporary Pagan chant, author unknown

The teachings of the minor arcana aren't really minor at all. Like a Native American medicine wheel or a Celtic circle of the seasons, each place on the wheel of fifty-six cards has its own unique gifts and challenges. These themes are seen through the number and element of each card. Aside from an intuitive reading of the picture itself, the querent or reader can easily discern a meaning for each card by meditating on the essence of the number and the symbolism of the element.

Elements: Air, Fire, Water, and Earth

The four elements have been known since ancient times as the building blocks of life. "Whether we see them as the breath, energy, blood, and body of the Mother, or as the blessed gifts of a Creator, or as symbols of the interconnected systems that sustain life, we know nothing can live without them," writes Starhawk in *The Fifth Sacred Thing*.[6] In the Gaian Tarot, the four suits correspond to each pure element with all their metaphors and symbolism.

Air, which corresponds to the suit of swords in most tarot decks, carries the qualities of thought, communication, ideas, clarity, words (spoken and written), making choices, the intellect, logic, problem-solving, learning, teaching, planning, intentions, intuition, prayers, and hope. Astrological air signs are Gemini, Libra, and Aquarius. Air speaks to us about the direction of East, the season of spring, and the crescent and first quarter moon phases.

Fire corresponds to the suit of wands. This element's themes are energy, passion, creativity, personal expression, sexuality, identity, power, personal will, actions, transformation, magic, inspiration, and enthusiasm. Astrological fire signs are Aries, Leo, and Sagittarius. Fire moves us in the direction of South, the season of summer, and the gibbous and full moon phases.

Water, the traditional suit of cups, embodies emotions (bliss, love, sorrow, joy, grief, disappointment), inner depths, dreams, fantasies, imagination, healing, spirituality, and mysticism. Astrological water signs are Pisces, Cancer, and Scorpio. Water reflects the direction

---

6.   Starhawk, *The Fifth Sacred Thing* (New York: Bantam, 1994), i.

of West, the season of autumn, and the disseminating and third quarter moon phases.

Earth parallels pentacles. It symbolizes the qualities of manifestation, stability, grounding, self-worth, values, practicality, health, prosperity, money, work, home, tradition, and security. Astrological earth signs are Capricorn, Taurus, and Virgo. Earth stands for the direction of North, the season of winter, and the balsamic (dark) and new moon phases.

Numbers: The Seeker's Journey through the Minors

Each of the number cards from the ace through the ten reflect the themes and wisdom of the corresponding major arcana card: Ace:Magician, 2:Priestess, 3:Gardener, and so on. The Seeker (Fool), numbered zero, is the querent's alter ego. Much has been written about the Fool's Journey through the majors, but there's a journey through the minors as well.

The Gaian Tarot's number system was inspired by Teresa Michelsen's work.[7] She views the minors as containing three sets of three-card mini-dramas, with the 10 as a card of transition. These sets are: Ace-2-3; 4-5-6; and 7-8-9. The first card of each set is a new beginning (ace, 4, 7). Each middle card (2, 5, 8) is a challenge card. The third card (3, 6, 9) is a resolution card, assuming

---

7.   Teresa Michelsen, *The Complete Tarot Reader: Everything You Need to Know from Start to Finish* (St. Paul, MN: Llewellyn, 2005).

the Seeker has successfully met the challenge of the middle card.

Each of the three sets of three goes a bit deeper as the Seeker grows and matures. The first triad parallels the trials and exploits of youth, roughly corresponding to the Child and Explorer people cards. The second triad is more about the experiences of midlife, corresponding to the Explorer and Guardian cards. The third triad is about maturity and wholeness, corresponding to the Guardian and Elder cards.

The challenge cards in each triad are specific: the 2 cards show a challenge of choice and the 5 cards depict a struggle with an external hardship. The 8 cards reflect the inner challenge of transforming one's vision or goal into a reality.

By the time the Seeker has reached the 9, she or he has been tested three times and has arrived at a level of accomplishment and maturity. With the 10 cards, the life cycle begins to transition to another turn on the Wheel. The tens are like a dark moon—something dies, and yet in that darkness, the new moon waits to be born. And the cycle begins again.

People: Children, Explorers, Guardians, and Elders

The people cards (court cards in traditional tarot decks) reflect four stages of life: childhood, early adulthood, midlife, and old age.

Children (pages) symbolize the qualities of discovery and birth. They are neophytes, students, or beginners in areas associated with their element. Each child is shown encountering a symbol of his or her suit for the first time—a butterfly, the flames of a campfire, a starfish at the tideline, and a just-picked apple. Children remind us of the sense of wonder we felt the first time we encountered the natural world close-up.

Explorers (knights) seek challenges and embody the principle of growth. They are driven by a quest or goal in areas associated with their element. The Explorers are all young adults, in their twenties and thirties. They are actively engaged in exploring the qualities of their suits. One is climbing a tree to see the full landscape, one is spinning fire, one is testing himself in an extreme sport, and one is an apprentice tracker.

Guardians (queens) represent the time of ripening or fruition. They are productive and actively involved in their communities. The Guardians are all at midlife, in their forties, fifties, or sixties. Each one "guards" or protects the qualities and issues defined by their suits. She is sitting in meditation, barefoot in the snow; he is tending the bonfire at a festival. She is pouring out the waters of mercy; he is nurturing the young corn plants in his garden.

Elders (kings) stand for dissemination and release. They are wise leaders and authority figures, and are respected in the communities. The Elders are seventy years and older. Because they are looking at the last phase of their lives, they take the long view. They are concerned with the wisdom of the ancestors as well as preparing the way for descendants yet to come. They pass on the wisdom of their respective suits. One brings peace through the sweet music of a flute, one casts a healing spell. One rows a boat out into the sound to greet the dawn, one spins wool into yarn even as she spins the destiny of the next generation.

Aces

Birth, Potential, Gift of Grace

The aces depict the birth of creatures who correspond to each element. A butterfly unfolds from a cocoon, a snake hatches from a leathery egg, a salmon fingerling begins to swim, a newborn fawn nestles under a cedar tree.

The ace begins the first of three triads in the number cards. Whatever process or drama begins with the ace is tested in the two, and resolved in the three.

The energy of an ace is similar to that of a new moon. It is a birth or rebirth; a seed or potential; a new opportunity or a new beginning, full of promise and hope. It is a gift of grace, the potency of the element coming to us at a particular moment in our lives when we need it the most.

It is more than a beginning, however, for the ace, (or number one), holds within itself a culmination or completion, a totality, the whole. A seed contains within itself the blueprint for an entire life cycle of birth, growth, blooming, release of seeds, withering, death, and rebirth. In the same way, the ace carries within itself the potential of the entire life cycle.

Ace Themes

- Beginning
- Opportunity
- Gift of Grace
- Conception
- Elemental Energy
- Potential
- Birth
- Seed
- Starting point

Ace of Air

A butterfly emerges from a chrysalis on a bright spring morning, with hawthorn (the "May-flower") in bloom. The butterfly is a symbol of the soul—*psyche* is the Greek word for both "soul" and "butterfly." Her ability to go through the process of metamorphosis speaks to your capacity to change yourself. A tincture of hawthorn berries supports blood and heart health, and heals our hearts in other ways as well. "Follow your heart," says Hawthorn. "You're a brand-new being," says Butterfly.

When you get this card in a reading...
You are emerging from a period of gestation, blossoming with new ideas, thoughts, or decisions. You may find it easy to change outmoded ideas, habits, or attitudes. Your mind is in harmony with your heart, and you are lighthearted, joyful, and beautiful.

When you read the Shadow side of this card...
You would prefer to stay warm and cozy in the chrysalis and not go through the coming metamorphosis. Your mind and heart are in disagreement. Your challenge is to find within yourself the determination to take flight.

Affirmation
I am blossoming with new ideas and decisions.

Ace of Fire

A snake has just broken his way out of an egg and is encountering the world for the first time. Because of his ability to shed his skin and grow into a new one, Snake has long been a symbol of renewal and transformation. In the background we see sparks shooting from a hidden flame, symbolizing the fires of creativity, sexuality, and empowerment.

When you get this card in a reading...
You are bursting with new energy! Your sense of self is heightened and you are feeling assertive. You are charged with creativity and can't wait to begin new projects. You may be discovering a new way of expressing your sexuality. You are beginning a transformation of some kind, and quite possibly a healing as well.

When you read the Shadow side of this card...
You are squelching the creative, passionate energy that wants to come forth. You are fearful of change and would prefer to stay as you are, even if you are unhappy. Your challenge is to find within yourself the courage to transform.

Affirmation
I am ablaze with creativity and passion!

Ace of Water

Salmon have spawned in a deep pool on the side of a river. Bright orange eggs are scattered among the rocks at the bottom of the pool. The just-hatched alevins and a salmon fingerling start to explore their watery world. Salmon's journey is one of descent and return, the archetypal shaman's journey. Salmon will travel hundreds of miles downstream to the ocean, then back again to the stream where she was born to give birth to the next generation. In Celtic mythology, Salmon is the embodiment of wisdom.

When you get this card in a reading...
It's time to follow your heart's desire, instincts, and intuition. Your heart is full and you desire connection with others in friendship, romance, or with compassion. You may be setting out on a pilgrimage or quest to find your own personal Holy Grail. Go with the flow of the river as it makes its way down to the sea. Trust the wisdom of your own heart.

When you read the Shadow side of this card...
You mistrust your emotions and intuition, and are putting limits on your dreams. You have many good reasons for why you just can't follow your heart's desire. Your challenge is to learn to trust your feelings and intuition.

Affirmation
I seek my heart's desire.

Ace of Earth

A newborn fawn nestles up against the base of a red cedar, surrounded by the unfolding spirals of young fiddlehead ferns. Deer are common yet magical animals, who have the reputation of being able to lead one into the Otherworld. Grown stags symbolize virility and strength, as well as the wildness of the woods. Of the four creatures depicted in the aces, only Fawn stays close to home for the first few days after birth, where its mother nurses it frequently.

When you get this card in a reading...
Something is manifesting in the physical world for you—perhaps good fortune or renewed health is coming your way. You are nurturing others, or receiving nurturance. The qualities of strength, grace, and stability begin to emerge for you. The spiral path between the physical world and the unseen world begins to unfold.

When you read the Shadow side of this card...
You are out of touch with your body or you are experiencing a lack of resources. You have trouble giving or receiving nourishment, and you don't believe you can find the path between this world and the Unseen. Your challenge is to find the strength within yourself to believe that good things can come your way.

Affirmation
I take root in the physical world.

Twos

Balance, Receptivity,
Attraction, Test of Choice

In the twos, a woman listens to the companion calls of birds, two fire dancers throw off sparks with their glances, a woman and dog share a cross-species embrace, and a young father balances his babies as he shops for dinner.

The two in each suit represents the first "test" in the number cards—it is one of choice.

The two cards express the energies of balance, polarity, attraction, and receptivity in their respective elemental suits. They also introduce the idea of duality: yin and yang, day and night, male and female, light and shadow. From the wholeness of one (the aces), comes two: me and you, the self and the not-self. There is awareness of the other; we are now in a relationship, and therefore choices and decisions must be made.

The two is related to the Priestess (major 2), with its themes of reflection, intuition, and receptivity.

Two Themes

- Balance
- Attraction
- Duality
- Choice

- Polarity
- Receptivity
- Reflection

Two of Air

A woman stands by a hawthorn tree in bloom, listening to two cedar waxwings making companion calls. She closes her eyes to shut out extraneous noises so she can hear the quietest bird call, the one behind all the other ones. She cradles something precious in her hands— perhaps a stone or broken bird's egg. It becomes a talisman of silence and awareness. "The quieter you become, the more you can hear," says Ram Dass.

When you get this card in a reading ...

You are learning to become so still that you can hear the quietest sound of all—the voice within your own heart, the voice of Spirit. Come into the awareness of silence and stillness. Make time and space in your day to sit in silence and allow insight to appear. When there are decisions to be made, it's best to "move at the pace of guidance," as Christina Baldwin says in *Seven Whispers*.

When you read the Shadow side of this card ...

You mind is so busy you can't discern the voice of guidance. It's time to slow down, take a walk, and listen to the birds and the beating of your own heart. Your challenge is to learn to be still enough to hear the voice of Spirit within.

Affirmation

I take time in my day to listen and be open to receiving insight.

Two of Fire

Two fire dancers, charged with sexual attraction, come close to embracing but hold themselves back. Their torches form a blazing "X" between them as their challenging gazes meet. Sparks fly. Will they or won't they?

When you get this card in a reading...
You are suddenly and passionately attracted to a person, idea, place, cause, or project. You are lit up with a blazing energy that makes your whole life sweeter. But you don't have to act on every instance of attraction. Will the fire warm you or burn you? It's time to choose; will you follow through on this attraction or not?

When you read the Shadow side of this card...
You are afraid to act on the attraction you feel, or you think you can't handle the life changes this choice will bring. Doubts creep in. It's possible the excitement is coming from a place of dysfunction. "No" may be the best response, but you must make your choice from a place of power, not from a place of fear. Your challenge is to find your place of power, and choose from there.

Affirmation
I am empowered by my passion for life, love, and wildness.

Two of Water

A woman and her canine friend joyfully embrace near a waterfall. The woman's heart chakra is tattooed with a design of an opening lotus. The waterfall creates negative ions, which refresh and uplift the spirit. Dog and human meet in a joyful heart connection, for dogs epitomize faithfulness, companionship, and unconditional love.

When you get this card in a reading...
You have a caring, compassionate response to another. You choose to begin or continue a relationship based on a deep heart connection, as you recognize and honor the Divine in each other. This connection brings healing and joy. Namaste—God/dess in me bows to God/dess in you.

When you read the Shadow side of this card...
You may feel deflated, as if all your joy is draining away. You may be experiencing unrequited or codependent love, or you may realize a relationship is at an end. Perhaps you fear sharing your heart with another. Your challenge is to keep your connection with Divine love clear and open, even when other relationships are troubling.

Affirmation
My heart is full and open, as I recognize the Divine in my beloved.

Two of Earth

A young father balances his baby sons in his arms as he shops for ingredients for the family's meal at the local market. One baby howls while the other is placid. The man compares prices and weighs options for dinner while simultaneously soothing one baby and hugging the other. The West African symbol on his T-shirt is an adinkra symbol of a crocodile, signifying the adaptability of living in water while breathing the air.

When you get this card in a reading…
You are balancing more than one thing at a time and adapting to a potentially chaotic situation. Your responsibilities may weigh heavily on you, or you may be handling them with grace. We tend to pride ourselves on how well we multitask, but it often comes at the price of losing our focus. Perhaps it's time to consider doing one thing at a time for a change.

When you read the Shadow side of this card…
You are having difficulty managing more than one thing at a time, and may become exasperated or lose your temper. You may have trouble making sound choices regarding health or money when your attention is pulled in another direction. Your challenge is to stay grounded and centered while adapting to a rapidly changing situation.

Affirmation
I stay centered in the midst of many demands on my time and attention.

Threes

Harmony, Flow, Abundance

In the threes, a young man pours out his thoughts on paper, a woman dances under a brilliant sunset, otters play in a kelp bed, and three women concoct herbal medicines while enjoying each other's company.

The three in each suit represents the resolution of the first three cards. Something began with the Ace, was tested in the two, and is manifested in the three.

The threes express the energies of abundance, harmony, and manifestation in each elemental suit. Three is a magical, mystical number that reflects the triplicity of God/dess (Maiden/Mother/Crone, Father/Son/Holy Spirit) in religious and esoteric symbolism. If card 1, the Magician, is pure male or yang energy and 2, the High Priestess, is pure female or yin energy, then 3 represents their union or the child they create together.

Three is related to the Gardener (major 3), with its themes of fertility, abundance, and pleasure.

Three Themes

- Harmony
- Ease
- Productivity
- Abundance
- Manifestation
- Expression

Three of Air

A man writes furiously in his journal, his thoughts and feelings pouring out onto the page. He may be working out issues that trouble him, reflected in the image that has turned up for his "card of the day" practice. Pen, pencil, and feather stand in a red glass jar, anchored in place by river stones. Behind him are shelves of books filled with ideas, inspiration, and wisdom.

When you get this card in a reading…
You are caught up in a whirlwind of thoughts and feelings, either positive or negative. What rushes through your mind? What ideas, memories, or scenes replay themselves in your head over and over again? Use the tools of the writer to release these ideas and emotions onto the page. Consider keeping a journal as a tool for self-exploration and understanding.

When you read the Shadow side of this card…
You may be stuck in a pattern of negative thinking and are so accustomed to it that you are finding it difficult to find your way out. Turn those negative thoughts around by keeping a gratitude journal. Each night before you go to bed, list at least three things you are grateful for. You'll find this simple tool to be a very powerful one. Your challenge is to break free of the trap of negative thinking.

Affirmation
Insights emerge as I document my thoughts and feelings as words.

Three of Fire

A woman dances with billowing scarves as a blazing sunset turns the evening sky into an inferno. She herself blazes as well, with passion and personal power. Her crackling, magical energy even draws three "great balls of fire" into her sphere.

When you get this card in a reading ...

You are on fire with the joy of creativity, sexuality, and self-empowerment. Nothing will hold you back from expressing yourself with great abandonment and rowdiness. This is no time to hide your light under a bushel. Be proud of who you are and what you've accomplished. It's an exciting time for you! Who knows where your passion, creativity, and magic will take you next?

When you read the Shadow side of this card ...

You are feeling self-conscious about expressing yourself. You may be just a little bit too modest for your own good. If you must dance alone, go ahead; but still get up and dance! This is not the time for inhibitions or restraint. Your challenge is to let go of self-doubt and let your brilliance shine in the world.

Affirmation

I express my joy and passion openly.

Three of Water

Three curious sea otters play in great forests of kelp. Two float on their backs on the surface of the water, chattering away. Another dives deep, perhaps going after shells he's just tossed in. Later on they'll swim to shore and find a place to slide down a muddy bank on their bellies. Otters seem to be carefree, mischievous creatures who enchant us humans with their antics and charm.

When you get this card in a reading...

It's time to seek joy in your life and share it with others. When we tell our friends and family about our happiness and invite them to be part of it, the happiness grows. So gather your friends together and go have some fun! Dive, swim, roll over, and play in the salty waters of Mama Ocean. And remember, as Thich Nhat Hanh said, "sometimes your joy is the source of your smile, but sometimes your smile can be the source of your joy." Smile and spread the joy around.

When you read the Shadow side of this card...

You may find it difficult to feel joyful about anything. It is possible however, to choose joy, even in difficult circumstances. Shift your energy with music, art, or being around people that lighten your spirit. Remember to ask for help if you need it. Learn to trust that loving support is available for you, even if you are hesitant to seek it. The joy you can tap into from within is the joy that will sustain you even in the roughest times. Your challenge is to allow this joy to flow freely, no matter what is happening around you.

Affirmation
I find joy in the company of others.

Three of Earth

Three women make tinctures, teas, salves, and other healing concoctions out of the herbs they've gathered in gardens and fields. They work joyfully together to create aromatic medicine for the good of the community. A traditional meaning for this card is "building the house of the Goddess." In this case, the temple of the Goddess is our own bodies, and the herbs nourish and sustain us.

When you get this card in a reading…
You are gathering in community with others to create something of lasting value. When we work together cooperatively, the final product is one of synergy—it is more than each of its separate parts. The pleasure we take in each other's company finds its way into the medicine we are creating. What wonderful gifts are you and your friends making for your community?

When you read the Shadow side of this card…
You may have not yet found a community where you feel at home. It's time to seek one out, or better yet, create one. Find others with mutual interests and start a gathering in your home or at a local bookstore. Relationships begin slowly and build over time. Your challenge is to reach out to others and find your community.

Affirmation
Where would I be without my tribe?

Fours

Sacred Space, Boundaries, Limits

In the fours, a bird's nest is hidden away from prying eyes, a woman celebrates herself in ritual space, another woman meditates by a sacred well, and a squirrel gathers acorns to stash away for the winter.

The four in each suit represents the beginning of the second triad of cards. A new drama or process begins; this one is on a deeper level than the drama of the Ace-2-3. In the three, we expanded; in the fours, we contract and build a foundation so we can move forward.

The four cards express the energies of structure, boundaries, and sacred space in each elemental suit. When we create sacred space, we acknowledge and honor the four directions—East, South, West, North. This centers us and creates a container for spiritual work. Limits and boundaries keep energies in as well as keeping unwanted energies out.

Four is related to the Builder (major 4), with its themes of structure, boundaries, and stewardship.

Four Themes

- Sacred space
- Boundaries
- Foundation

- Structure
- Limits
- Stewardship

Four of Air

Four robin's eggs are nestled inside a nest fashioned from twigs, grasses, moss, flower petals, and bits of ribbon and string. It's hidden away, tucked under leaves that protect it from prey or prying eyes.

When you get this card in a reading…
It's time to create a sacred space for rest, retreat, prayer, and meditation. Take time out to dream, incubate your ideas and get your mind clear. Keep your boundaries firm and strong—if your nest falls apart, the incubating energy inside is destroyed. During your "time out," you may want to keep your special place hidden and safe. Be wary of predators (including inner ones) who may be ready to snatch away your time alone, personal space, or ideas.

When you read the Shadow side of this card…
You are unable or unwilling to take some time for yourself. Perhaps you worry that your family or work colleagues won't be able to function without you. Perhaps you think you don't deserve what you have. Or perhaps outer circumstances seem to be conspiring against you, because of your many responsibilities. Your challenge is to make time for yourself. It it utterly necessary for your well-being.

Affirmation
I take time to get away to my own little nest where I incubate new ideas and dreams.

Four of Fire

A woman stands within a sacred circle, the four directions marked by tall votive candles. She is breathing deeply, allowing the energy of the desert night to flood her body. Energy moves up from the earth and down from the sky into her body. Kundalini rises, power flows, all blocks are gone. She is marking a personal rite of passage and exulting in her own empowerment.

When you get this card in a reading...
You are celebrating your sense of personal power. When your body is humming with energy inside ritual space, you know you can do anything. Set your intent and follow through. Step into the sacred circle to celebrate a rite of passage, do a self-blessing or create an act of magic. You have the power!

When you read the Shadow side of this card...
You feel depleted and worn out and are buffeted about by others' decisions and whims. You need to celebrate and take a stand for yourself. You are strong and beautiful—don't you forget it! Your challenge is to find your inner power and celebrate it.

Affirmation
I am strong and courageous, and have the power to accomplish anything I choose to do.

Four of Water

A young woman gazes into the waters of Chalice Well, a holy well in Glastonbury, England. Is she sad and grieving? Is she at peace? She may be scrying the patterns on the surface of the water, or contemplating the mysteries of the red waters. The Lady of the Well murmurs secrets in her ear as she gazes at the water. If her own personal well is empty and in need of replenishment, it will be filled to overflowing in this sacred place.

When you get this card in a reading...

It's time to replenish your emotional reserves. Spending time near a body of water cleanses and purifies us, whether it's a beach, riverbank, or sacred well. You may want to make a pilgrimage to a sacred place near your home or far away. If you do, remember to take along an offering for the guardian spirits. By honoring them, you open the way to receiving their blessings.

When you read the Shadow side of this card...

You may feel drained and empty, as if your own personal well has run dry. You may feel bored, lethargic, or emotionally unstable. You may not appreciate the blessings in your life. It's time to turn all that around. Go to the water, even if it's your own bathtub. Allow the water to wash away your troubles. Your challenge is to find a way to come into emotional balance.

Affirmation

I allow the sacred waters to pour peace and contentment into me.

Four of Earth

On a beautiful autumn day, a grey squirrel pauses to nibble on an acorn as he gathers nuts and seeds to save for the winter to come. He is surrounded by a stash of acorns, and even more tumble out of an opening in the trunk of a maple tree. In Inuit culture, an *inukshuk* (much like a cairn) of stacked stones often signifies safety, hope, and friendship—all qualities that can't be hoarded. Here, the four stones represent an embodied prayer.

When you get this card in a reading...
You are building a structure for personal safety and security, wisely stewarding your resources. In times of plenty, you're saving up for the lean times ahead. You may want to start a practice of building blessing cairns. Each stone can represent something you're grateful for; the stack is a physical gratitude list! They can also represent prayers you say as you stack the stones. The stones remind us of our connection to All That Is, and to our soul's purpose.

When you read the Shadow side of this card...
You might ask yourself if you are taking or using more than your fair share. Our friend Squirrel can become so acquisitive that he saves more food than he really needs. He sometimes forgets all the places where he hoarded his food for the winter. What is the best use of your

resources? Your challenge is to make use of them in a way that is sustainable.

Affirmation

I'm a wise steward of my resources and I give thanks for the blessings in my life.

Fives

Challenge, Change, Test of Hardship

In the fives, eagles fight for territory, a man breathes a ball of fire into the air, a woman gazes longingly through the fog, and a hiker settles down to wait out a storm.

The five in each suit represents a crisis or test of hardship from the outside world.

The five cards express the energies of challenge and conflict in each elemental suit. After the stability (and sometimes rigidity) of the fours, our world is shaken up by the fives. This is usually involuntary change; we're content with our lives but a crisis is thrust upon us. This change is often traumatic because it is unexpected.

The five is related to the Teacher (major 5). Life lessons are sometimes quite painful, but often lead to spiritual growth.

Five Themes

- Challenge
- Conflict
- Change
- Crisis
- Instability

Five of Air

Five bald eagles scream and fight over territory. Once an endangered species, the 1972 ban on DDT resulted in a big comeback for eagles. In some areas, the resurgence has led to overpopulation and competition for habitat. Visitors to the wilderness may even witness eagles fighting to the death.

When you get this card in a reading...
You are involved in a turf battle or argument that has become quite nasty. Bitter words, gossip, and slander may be thrown about. Unwelcome criticism may be given or received. Your opponents may be family members, friends, coworkers, or "the system." Is there a way to defend your territory without attacking others? Conflicts often generate growth, as painful as they might be. What can you learn from the present conflict about the power of words?

When you read the Shadow side of this card...
You may have internalized all the negative words and attitudes that come from others. Doing so can even cause you to become lost in negative self-talk, to the point that the conflict is now entirely in your head. If so, you need to recognize and release it. On the other hand, you may be the instigator of hostilities. In what ways might you be at fault? Are you willing to take responsibility for your words and actions? Alternatively,

you may have begun to consider ways to solve the dispute: compromise, cooperation, reconciliation.

Affirmation

I defend my own place in the world without resorting to bitterness or hurtful words.

Five of Fire

A fire performer spits billowing flames out of his mouth. Twisted faces of gargoyles or maddened creatures form in the smoke and fire. Breathing fire can burn both the performer and his audience. It's powerful, exciting, and potentially lethal.

When you get this card in a reading...

You are playing a dangerous game. You like being the center of attention and are tempted to dominate those around you. You may be venting your rage by letting it all out, not caring who might get burned. You may be acting like a "hot head"—short-tempered and easily set off. Or you may enjoy testing yourself by "playing with fire." Rage and anger are often masks for that which we fear, represented by the frightening faces in the smoke. "We can let the circumstances of our lives harden us so that we become increasingly resentful and afraid," says the Dalai Lama. "Or we can let them soften us and make us kinder. We always have the choice."

When you read the Shadow side of this card...

You either sink deeper into anger, despair, and burnout, or the fire serves as a catalyst to wake you up and turn you in a new direction. In that case, the fire becomes a symbol of courage, transformation, and liberation. Which will it be for you?

Affirmation

I courageously face my fears.

Five of Water

A woman sits on a misty shore, wrapped up against the cold. She holds a scrying bowl in her hands but no images have arisen in it. Her longing gaze is directed inwardly as the fog of depression descends over the scene. In the distance, a boat is moored to the shore.

When you get this card in a reading...
You are hovering on the edge of grief, despondency, or discouragement. You may be regretting lost opportunities or missing someone terribly. Depression has been called "anger turned inward," yet also "intuition unheeded." How might you reclaim your neglected intuitive abilities? What message do you need to receive from your intuition? It can be hard to find a way out of the gloom, and yet it is not impossible. There's a boat in the distance that will take you through the mists to the farther shore. What is on the other side?

When you read the Shadow side of this card...
You may fall deeper into depression and despondency, refusing to move beyond grief or disappointment. Being sad may have become a habit that's hard to break. Alternatively, you may find the courage to paddle out of the fog into renewal and recovery. There will always be those who are willing to help you, but you must make the choice to heal yourself.

Affirmation
I will let healing flow through me and move me out of depression.

Five of Earth

A hiker finds himself lost in the deep woods when a storm blows in. He builds a debris hut and hunkers down inside it to wait out the night. Even though he's cold and uncomfortable, he knows he has the skills he needs to survive and make it safely out of the wilderness once the storm has passed.

When you get this card in a reading...

You are dealing with stress on a survival level, most likely with your health or finances. You may have lost your home or your job, or are dealing with a life-threatening illness. Things may seem bleak indeed. What kind of "shelter in the storm" can you create that will help you through these rough times? What survival skills have you developed that you can use in times of crisis?

When you read the Shadow side of this card...

You may be caught up in scarcity consciousness, or are giving in to the worst fears that arise in the middle of the night. You don't see a way out and don't trust your own ability to get through the crisis. You might be looking down on others who are experiencing misfortune, "blaming the victim" and assuming they brought it on themselves through actions or karma. If you are the one in trouble, ask for help. When you see others in trouble, lend a helping hand.

Affirmation

I have the skills it takes to survive any crisis.

Sixes

Community, Reciprocity, Peak Experience

In the sixes, friends gather to greet a new day, drummers and dancers raise energy by a festival bonfire, sisters circle in the gentle waves of Mama Ocean, and money is exchanged for flowers and vegetables at a farmers' market.

The six in each suit represents the resolution of the crisis of the five, and depicts a happy experience shared with others. The six is the completion of the second triad in the number cards.

The six cards express the qualities of community, reciprocity, and peak experience in their respective elemental suits. The happiness and fulfilment we experience in the Sixes give us the self-confidence and energy to move on to the next phase in our lives, represented by the third triad of 7-8-9.

Six is related to the Lovers (major 6) with its themes of love, bliss, and unity.

Six Themes

- Reciprocity
- Peak experience
- Community
- Collaboration
- Interaction

Six of Air

The community awakens and "sings up the sun" together with prayer, song, and drumming. As we gather with others of like mind at festivals or on retreat, we gain perspective and insight into the big, soulful issues of our lives. As we set our intent together in ceremonial space, the power to change our personal and planetary lives is magnified many times over.

When you get this card in a reading ...

You are gaining clarity and insight by spending time with others of like mind. You may be setting an intent for change in your personal life or the life of the planet, and are being supported in that intent by others. The saying goes, "You can't make room for the New in your life until you're grateful for what you already have." By cultivating a practice of gratitude, we make room for the Great Mystery to respond in kind.

When you read the Shadow side of this card ...

You may be finding it difficult to find anything to be grateful for, and your mind may be foggy or confused. You may be looking for the worst side of every situation or caught up in a cycle of negative thinking. It might be a good idea to get away with your friends where you'll find new perspectives on the issues that are troubling you.

Affirmation

I greet the new day with a song in my heart.

Six of Fire

It's festival time! With nightfall comes the lighting of the bonfire and the arrival of drummers and dancers. The energy builds until it reaches a blazing peak of creative and erotic power, and we are entrained and entranced. Together we fan the flames of the sacred fire. We raise a cone of power and release it—and are left utterly transformed.

When you get this card in a reading...
You are raising energy with others for magic, healing, and transformation. You may be experiencing an altered sense of reality, or are charged with power at the center of the circle. You are playing your own instrument and making your own unique contribution to the communal dance. Celebrate—dance to the music!

When you read the Shadow side of this card...
You may be burned out and exhausted, and fearful of joining with others in a sacred dance. You may feel you have nothing to offer. Your inner fire is burning weakly and you need to be revitalized. Seek out the people and places that will ignite your fire once again.

Affirmation
I passionately celebrate myself and my tribe!

Six of Water

"Mermaid" sisters gather together to celebrate the peak of summer as sunset falls on the longest day of the year. They are naked and innocent, with hearts wide open to embrace each other. They weave a sensuous, spellbinding web of love and pleasure as they sing, "we are the flow, we are the ebb..." They slip between the borders of earth and sea, night and day, human and fish—to the place where magic begins.

When you get this card in a reading...

You are opening your heart to close connections and joy as you circle with beloved friends. You bless yourself and each other as you are rocked and nurtured by Mama Ocean. Your tribe expands to include the four-legged, winged, finned, and flippered ones. At this magic time, you are fully in the present moment, having left all cares and worries behind.

When you read the Shadow side of this card...

You may long to be part of a sisterhood, or you may be nostalgically looking back on a time in your life when you were part of a community. You may be brooding on the past or worrying about the future, and finding it difficult to stay centered in the present moment. Call your community to you, even if you don't yet know who they are. Go to the water and cast your prayer upon the waves.

Affirmation

I open my heart to all my relations and honor our connection.

Six of Earth

At a local farmers' market, vendors and customers exchange energy in the tangible form of money for goods. We buy our greens and carrots from the farmer who lives down the road and in doing so support her commitment to farming organically and sustainably. In return, we receive fresh and delicious foods that nourish our bodies and spirits. Sometimes we get stories with our groceries—of the toddler who helped pick those golden flowers; of the big rain that almost wiped out the tomato crop; or of long days spent in fragrant lavender fields. This is soulful shopping indeed.

When you get this card in a reading...
You are part of the cycle of giving and receiving. You happily exchange your hard-earned cash for goods that will enrich your body and spirit. You present your own gift to the community—the work of your hands and heart—and are pleased to find it so well-received. Your generosity and support of others circles back to you, and increases your own prosperity and health.

When you read the Shadow side of this card...
You may be in debt or are experiencing a lack of abundance in your life. You may not know how to spread the word about the brilliant work you do. You may be working too hard for very little return. It's time to make some adjustments in your relationship with money. You deserve to be well paid for the work of your heart and

hands. More importantly, your community needs the gift that only you can bring.

Affirmation

I appreciate and support the work of others, just as they support and appreciate me.

Sevens

Focus on a Goal, Inner Work

In the sevens, a hiker studies a map, a blacksmith works at a forge, a man drinks from a cup, and a woman plants a cedar sapling near a stream.

The seven in each suit begins the third triad and, like the ace and four, marks a beginning. The third cycle is the deepest of the three, representing a conscious choice and an initiation. We choose a field of study or a personal challenge that will move us into deeper self-knowledge.

The seven cards express the qualities of focus, setting intentions, and inner work. We've reached a level of success in the world and now have the maturity and self-confidence necessary to explore new territory. We realize that we want to live a life of purpose and seek to find out what that might mean. Even outer challenges resonate with inner meaning as we reflect on our place in the world and what we stand for.

Seven is related to the Chariot (major 7) with its themes of self-mastery, focus, and success.

Seven Themes

- Initiation
- Inner work
- Self-awareness
- Focus
- Setting intentions

Seven of Air

A hiker has paused on his journey to consult his map and to consider his destination. He needs to make plans for the next stage of his walkabout. Shall he climb the mountain or follow the river down into the valley? Shall he seek the company of others or continue to go it alone? Shall he take a shortcut, even though he might get stuck in the swamp of despair? What inner journey does this outer journey symbolize? He makes his plans and his strategies and—if he's wise—he leaves room for serendipity.

When you get this card in a reading...
It is time to strategize, plan, and prepare to move in a new direction. When we examine a map and consider all the alternate routes we might take, the map itself begins to form our worldview. We might stop to consider these questions: What has been left off the map? Is something there that we haven't noticed before? What landscape lays just beyond the edge of the map? At some point, we need to fold up the map and get back on the path.

When you read the Shadow side of this card...
You may feel stuck, as though you can't move unless you have planned for every possible contingency. Or you may be stumbling around without a plan, flitting here and there without making any progress. Clarify your goal and start taking steps towards it. Plans and

strategies are important but will only take us so far. Trust the journey and the lessons that may come along the way.

Affirmation
I make my plans but leave room for serendipity.

Seven of Fire

A blacksmith stands at a forge, raising her hammer high to strike the red-hot iron rod. The scent of rain-soaked autumn woods mixes with the pungent aroma of burning coals and hot metal. The smith's heartbeat races as she pounds the glowing iron bar into the shape she desires. It takes much strength and determination to bend iron to your will. The smith wears an amulet in the shape of Thor's hammer (Mjöllnir) around her neck. She draws on the power of the Viking god of thunder, as sparks like lightning fly from her hammer. She knows that nothing can keep her from accomplishing her desire.

When you get this card in a reading…
It's time for you to take a risk for personal growth and stand up for your authentic self. Dare to forge ahead! You are learning to trust your own strength and sense of personal power. You are expressing yourself creatively. And of course, you must "strike while the iron is hot"! Don't pass an opportunity by when it presents itself, for that's when transformation can occur.

When you read the Shadow side of this card…
You may be living according to the expectations of others, and may be having a hard time standing up for your beliefs and values. You may not recognize opportunities when they appear, or you may let them pass you by.

Your task is to find the inner strength you need to live an authentic life.

Affirmation

I have the courage and strength to transform my life.

Seven of Water

A man has chosen one dream out of many possible dreams. He has let go of dithering over this fantasy or that option and has made his choice. It's the moment of commitment for him. Perhaps he listened when a wise one encouraged him: "Say no to the good, in order to say yes to the great."

When you get this card in a reading ...
It's time for you to narrow down your options and choose one dream or fantasy out of many. Saying no is as empowering as saying yes. What will open up for you as a result of this decision? Follow your intuition and lift that cup. Drink deeply, and let your well be filled.

When you read the Shadow side of this card ...
You may feel paralyzed and unable to choose between many options available to you. Choose to take action, even if you're uncertain. Making a decision to move forward sets you in motion. You can always change course later, but taking action will break you out of your paralysis.

Affirmation
I open my whole heart to my dream.

Seven of Earth

A woman plants a red cedar sapling near a creek where salmon spawn. She is volunteering for a habitat restoration project in an area that was once heavily logged. Alder trees have since sprung up, working to restore the land to health by breathing nitrogen into their leaves and transferring it into the soil. But it is time to replace them with water-loving cedar trees which will shade the creek so salmon can return from the ocean, spawn, and thrive for centuries. The Western red cedar can live for 1,500 years, grow to a width of 25 feet around, and reach a height of 250 feet. When cedars are planted in healthy soils, under the shade of other trees, they grow slow and strong, providing the best wood for building homes, boats, baskets, clothing, deep-sea fishing rope, and other necessities vital for life.

When you get this card in a reading …
It may be time to set a goal for yourself that involves long-term planning on a practical level. Don't expect to see results immediately, but be content to know that you are working slowly and steadily toward your goal. Be patient. You're not on your own timeline here—instead, you're on Mother Earth's schedule. You are learning to live in sync with her rhythms and cycles. Trust that your efforts are worthwhile, even if you don't see the fruits of your labors for a very long time—like a red cedar sapling reaching toward the sky,

transforming a clearcut into a temperate old growth rainforest.

When you read the Shadow side of this card ...
You may be feeling impatient, anxious, or frustrated about meeting your goal. You may want instant gratification instead of allowing the process to unfold and mature in its own good time. Take pleasure in daily progress, no matter how small it may seem. Learn to be patient. Slow down.

Affirmation
I trust that my efforts are growing to fruition in their own good time.

Eights

Taking Action, Challenge of
Transforming Vision into Reality

In the eights, a small group of people sit in a circle holding council, meteors streak across the sky, a woman swims against the current, and a father teaches his daughter to drum.

The eight in each suit illustrates the challenge of taking action in the world to make our dreams a reality. It is the final of three challenges.

The eight cards express the qualities of movement, self-empowerment and making our dreams come true. This challenge is a significant one. We chose in the sevens to explore our own inner depths and find how we might live a life of purpose. In the eights, we discover whether or not our choice will take root in the world. The number eight is drawn in the shape of a lemniscate, or eternity symbol, and there are eight spokes on the Wheel of the Year, symbolizing wholeness. If we meet the challenge of the eight, we will come into the fullness and completion of the nine.

Eight is related to Strength (major 8) with its themes of vitality, courage, and fortitude.

Eight Themes

- Taking action
- Energy
- Self-directed movement
- Empowerment
- Transforming vision into reality

Eight of Air

A small group of people sit in a circle, holding council. One man is talking while the others are actively listening. Perhaps they are planning a political action, remembering the words of Margaret Mead: "Never doubt the ability of a small group of concerned citizens to change the world." Perhaps they are working to achieve consensus on an issue that is important to their bonds as a spiritual circle. Maybe they are a peer counseling group. Or they could be participating in the deep transformation that can happen when we tell our authentic stories, and others listen deeply from their hearts.

When you get this card in a reading ...

You are being challenged to transform your vision into reality with a little help from your friends. In a circle, everyone shares power and no one is "above" anyone else. It may be a struggle to co-create a vision with others, and it may be hard on the individual ego to reach consensus in a group. But oh, the rewards! May we all learn to give good attention to others, and listen deeply and well.

When you read the Shadow side of this card ...

You may feel discouraged about making a difference in the world. You may feel jaded or burned out from working with others in a group process. You may be tempted to go it alone. Perhaps you should ask yourself what you can do to support the visions of the group.

Affirmation
We see it, so be it!

Eight of Fire

Meteors with trails like sparkling diamonds streak swiftly towards the earth. Meteor showers are spectacular sights that fill our hearts with awe and wonder. The ancients believed they were portents of great change, for good or ill.

When you get this card in a reading…

Are you missing the spectacular show in the night sky because your attention is elsewhere? Stay open to inspiration, and when it strikes, act quickly before it fades away! Let the meteor showers inspire you to burn brightly and move swiftly, as you take action towards making your visions a reality.

When you read the Shadow side of this card…

You may be set in your ways and resisting change, or you may be panicking in the face of too much change. Perhaps you are rushing others. You may have forgotten to be looking and listening for inspiration.

Affirmation

I act quickly when inspiration strikes.

Eight of Water

A woman swims upstream in a river, intent on reaching her destination. She is focused and determined, as she takes action to live an authentic life. There may be times when she feels like she's in over her head, when she wants to turn around and let the current take her swiftly and easily downstream. But then she'll just have to pick herself up and head upstream again, after having lost a lot of ground. "Stay true to yourself," the river whispers. "Keep to your course 'til you make landfall."

When you get this card in a reading...
You are taking action to live authentically, even though it is very difficult to go against the current at times. The current itself may symbolize an outmoded way of doing things that no longer serves you. It may represent mainstream, conformist values and standards that discourage you from living your life in a more unique way. You may feel that your past is holding you back, but you can leave the past behind. You have the courage, strength, and determination to reach your destination.

When you read the Shadow side of this card...
The past may feel like it is overwhelming you, or you may feel like it is too hard to change the way you live. In the end, though, living an inauthentic life is more painful than the struggle to swim upstream. You can do it!

Affirmation
I embrace my own true path.

Eight of Earth

Like a master craftsman and his apprentice, a father teaches his young daughter to drum. He is a mentor and role model to her, and the devotion between them seals the lessons of rhythm and tempo. As she learns the intricacies of drumming, she cultivates patience, as skill is developed over many long hours of practice. The love and respect between a drummer and his drum is echoed in the love and respect between father and daughter, teacher and student.

When you get this card in a reading...

A long apprenticeship is sometimes required when we work to manifest our vision in the world. We must learn our craft and practice it diligently, reaching a high level of skill, before we can walk the path of right livelihood. What is the work of your heart? And have you found a mentor who will teach you wisely? And will you pass on your knowledge to another?

When you read the Shadow side of this card...

You may not be ready or willing to put in the long hours of practice and training required to become skilled at any craft or profession. Or you may be frustrated because you have not found a mentor or a way to share your gifts. What can you do to share your brilliance with the world?

Affirmation

I cultivate patience as I learn so that I may share my gifts with others.

Nines

Solitude, Mastery, Wisdom

In the nines, a woman releases her grief, a man sits in deep meditation, one woman has an ecstatic experience in a sea cave, and another woman enjoys a beautiful day in a field of lavender.

The nine in each suit represents the end of the third of three cycles, and is the most powerful card of completion. The power of "three times three" is the most potent of all. The figures in these cards are all experiencing the abundance and satisfaction of completing this cycle.

The nine cards depict the qualities of solitude, experience, and wisdom as seen through the elemental suits. In these cards, we have reached a level of self-mastery, peace, and wisdom that has been hard-won. More than any other cards, they represent the ability to live in the present moment.

Nine is related to the Hermit (major 9) with its themes of solitude, soul-searching, and wisdom.

Nine Themes

- Self-mastery
- Wisdom
- Completion
- Solitude
- Experience

On a much deeper soul level than the distress of the Three of Air, a woman grieves. Storm clouds billow behind her, mirroring her inner turmoil. Yet she has gone to a sacred spot, and embraces a standing stone as if it were her mother. She goes deep into a trance state, letting her sorrow ground into the body of the earth. And with her inner vision she sees the face of She Who Watches—the One who always watches over her with love and compassion. (Note: She Who Watches is a petroglyph found near the Columbia River on the border of Washington and Oregon.)

When you get this card in a reading...
Deep sorrow has come into your life and your mind swirls with nightmare images. Grief can be exhausting, especially when we think of all the "could have's" and "should have's." Release your sorrow into the earth, the body of the Mother, where it is grounded and transformed. You know the Compassionate One is always there to comfort you.

When you read the Shadow side of this card...
You may be allowing your grief to crush you, or you may be unwilling to face your fears. You may be lost in depression. Only you can know when you are ready to heal and move on. Allow the sorrow that you have known to give you more empathy and compassion for others.

Affirmation
I allow the Mother to heal my sorrow as I open my
heart in compassion to others.

Nine of Fire

A man has retreated to a red rock cave, a sacred spot where energies gather, in order to replenish his own life-force. He seats himself in meditation; soon the kundalini serpent begins to rise. He radiates inner fire, connected to heaven and earth. He experiences himself as a being of light, as well as a being of flesh, blood, and bone.

When you get this card in a reading ...
You have reached a time in your life when you are self-confident, self-possessed, and at peace with yourself. You are radiant with personal power and yet are humble and approachable. You use your personal power responsibly and competently. Because of your spiritual practice, you are able to handle anything that comes your way with calm equanimity.

When you read the Shadow side of this card ...
You may feel disconnected to the great power source of All That Is. It is time to start (or begin again) some kind of spiritual practice. There are many to choose from; try several out, then stick with the one that works best for you.

Affirmation
I am a being of light and fire, as well as flesh and bone.

Nine of Water

A woman enters a sacred sea cave and lifts her arms to receive the embrace of the Ocean Mother. She sings a song of devotion as waves crash and salt spray kisses her brow. As she sings in harmony with the rushing wind and the tide, she enters into a mystical state of ecstasy. When she leaves, she gathers nine white stones that carry the energy of the cave and the song she sang to the Mother.

When you get this card in a reading...

This is a time of emotional fulfillment, dreams manifested, mystical experience, and connection to Spirit. What song of praise fills your heart at this time? You are overflowing with joy and peace. All is well.

When you read the Shadow side of this card...

You have shut down your senses and have forgotten how to open up to the Divine. You may be looking for your happiness in material possessions but are never satisfied, no matter how much you have. You may be feeling smug about your success and your possessions. Dive deep into your heart to know what will bring you true and lasting happiness.

Affirmation

True happiness is found in my connection to Spirit.

Nine of Earth

A woman stands in the midst of a lavender field in full bloom on a sacred island where she has put down roots and made her home. She's reached a time in her life when she is fulfilled, content, and at peace with her home and her creative work. Even when she spends time in sacred solitude, she is inextricably part of a community that includes the people, plants, and animals who call this place home. Sister Heron flies overhead, a sign to her of the presence of the Divine in her life.

When you get this card in a reading...
You're enjoying a time of accomplishment and comfort. You're at the peak of your creative powers, and are well-paid for your work. You are connected to your family and community, yet have time alone for creative and spiritual pursuits. It is a time of peace and plenty in your life, both internal and external.

When you read the Shadow side of this card...
You may not yet have experienced peace and plenty, and you may not yet have found your heart's home. You may be restless and unsatisfied, even if you have an abundant lifestyle. Consider what you need to be truly secure and prosperous, then recognize how much you already have.

Affirmation
I am grateful for the place I call home.

Tens

Transition

In the tens, Canada geese fly south in the fall migration, a forest fire rages, salmon spawn and die in a mountain stream, and new growth emerges from a decaying stump in the woods.

The ten in each suit is a card of endings, with an implicit new beginning encoded within. This is the place where we pause to look back on the three cycles of three just completed, and the life experiences that have molded our characters. We also look ahead to the next Ace and the beginning of another cycle.

The ten cards depict the qualities of transition and transformation as seen through the elemental suits. The energy of a ten is like a balsamic moon phase, when all seems to be darkness and decay. Yet a new moon is only hours away and the round will soon begin again.

Ten is related to the Wheel (major 10) with its themes of cycles, flux, and transition.

Ten Themes

- Transition
- Endings and beginnings

- Transformation

Ten of Air

Canada geese fly in a V-formation during the fall migration. We can almost hear the chorus of honking. The familiar sight of geese flying south for the winter never fails to tug at our hearts, bringing a sense of impermanence and longing. According to Japanese folklore, a person who sees a flock of birds overhead might suddenly yearn to travel. In European tales of the Wild Hunt, it was said that flocks of wild geese or swans embodied the souls of the dead who flew through the winter night sky.

When you get this card in a reading ...
It's a bittersweet time of letting go. You may not want to face the winter to come, yet it is inevitable. What plans, ideas or strategies do you need to release as the old year wanes? Are you longing to wander away from your present circumstances? Which ancestors whisper to you as the geese fly overhead? What wisdom do they have for you?

When you read the Shadow side of this card ...
You may be resisting the progress of time and want to hold on to an endless summer. This is not the way of things, as we all know. Surrendering to the natural flow will lead to the discovery of treasures that are only found during the times of cold and dark.

Affirmation

I heed the inevitability of change and discover the gifts found in letting go.

Ten of Fire

A forest fire is raging, the smoke and ashes release into the air. To our "civilized" minds, a fire is terrifying because it's a threat to our homes, towns, animals, and possibly our lives. But forest fires are a natural part of the cycle of life, and were sometimes carefully set by indigenous people. Fire is necessary to clear away undergrowth and debris and is important to a forest's overall health. Fires are beneficial for prairies, which may need fire to maintain their very existence, and to some species such as the Lodgepole Pine, whose cones often need exposure to high temperatures in order to release their seeds.

When you get this card in a reading...
Does it feel like your dreams have gone up in smoke? Are you overwhelmed or burdened by loss? Remember that new seedlings grow and flourish in the ashes of a spent fire. You must release your passions and your energies, whether or not you want to, whether or not you think you're ready. It's time.

When you read the Shadow side of this card...
You can only focus on the devastation and loss, and see no hope for the future. This is a time for trust and for patience, until you see the seedlings emerge from the ashes.

Affirmation
I release what is finished, and clear the way for rebirth.

Ten of Water

The salmon cycle of descent and return is one of the most inspiring stories found in nature, whether you approach it as pure science or as a spiritual metaphor. Very simply, salmon fry are born in fresh water and are carried downriver to the sea where they grow to maturity. If they're not eaten by orca whales or caught by fishermen, they make their way back upriver to the same place they were hatched. Just as their bodies grew when they first floated downstream, their bodies transform again as they work their way upstream to spawn, laying eggs that will become the next generation. Then they die. Their bodies rot, and what isn't picked over by ravens and eagles is composted into the soil, turning it into fertile ground.

When you get this card in a reading...
You know that you are part of the great cycle of descent and return. You may identify with the courage of the salmon, whose struggle benefits the whole ecosystem as well as the next generation of salmon. How are you willing to struggle to improve the future for your family or community? Where in the cycle of loss, change, and increase do you find yourself at this time? Are you finding your way to your true home or your journey's completion?

When you read the Shadow side of this card...
You may be overwhelmed by emotions and are having difficulty functioning in the everyday world. Or you may feel like a martyr whose struggles go unappreciated by others. Ask for the help you need to return to a place of balance.

Affirmation
I have given my best and can rest knowing that love will continue to flow.

Ten of Earth

In the deep forest, we come across a "nurse stump" or "nurse log," a tree that has fallen during a storm or been cut down. As the log decays, it provides fertile ground for new growth to take root in its dying body. Insects and fungi hurry along the decomposition process. Squirrels and other creatures may perch or roost there, adding food scraps and scat to the rich humus. Soon moss, ferns and mushrooms appear, and the seedlings of new trees. Many years later, you will see full grown trees whose roots have grown over one of these nurse stumps or logs. In the background, an elderly gentleman walks the forest path through dappled shade and sunshine, heading for the spot that opens up into the light. So do we pass along our wisdom to the next generation, that they might flourish as we pass on.

When you get this card in a reading...
Something you thought had ended in your life is beginning to burst forth with new shoots. Perhaps it is the wisdom of your parents and your ancestors that you pass along to those who come after you. It may also be that the long journey to see your work succeed is finally paying off. What do you consider to be great wealth? It has been said that "what we have done for ourselves alone dies with us; what we have done for others and the world remains, and is immortal." (Albert Pike) In what ways does your work support and sustain others?

When you read the Shadow side of this card...
Have you allowed overwork and overwhelm to trap you? Perhaps you fear there is never enough for all, or you could lose all you have gained. In what ways might you be struggling with outmoded family expectations or social class prejudices? Our Mother Earth herself is the example of plentifulness, diversity, and sustainability. Be willing to let go of your demands, and allow her to bless you with the abundance you most need.

Affirmation
I know my life's work will benefit coming generations.

Children

Learning, Wondering, Beginning

Each child is shown encountering a symbol of his or her suit for the first time—a butterfly, the flames of a campfire, a starfish at the tideline, a just-picked apple. These children remind us of the sense of wonder we felt the first time we encountered the natural world close-up.

The children correspond to pages in traditional decks. In readings, children are neophytes, students, or beginners in areas associated with their element. They discover and observe and are open to new possibilities. Traditionally, they have also been seen as messengers. In a life cycle, they represent the quality of birth, corresponding to a new or crescent moon. Child cards can be read as another person, an aspect of yourself, or the quality of being child-like and having a "beginner's mind."

Child of Air

The Child of Air gazes at a swallowtail butterfly that alights on her hand as butterflies take flight in a spiral around her. She can feel the trembling of delicate wings and wonders if it's really a faery, disguised as a butterfly. Perhaps, like the Zen master Chuang-tzu, she asks: "Am I a person dreaming I'm a butterfly, or am I a butterfly dreaming I'm a person?"

When you get this card in a reading…
The Child of Air brings fresh insight to old situations in a light-hearted or whimsical way. Someone is very curious and may begin a new course of study or explore new points of view. This child is a sponge for soaking up new information, and her mind is sharp, alert, alive. She has discovered the secret of staying in the present moment (or perhaps it has discovered her).

When you read the Shadow side of this card…
Someone is afraid to explore new ideas or make changes, perhaps because of critical voices. It's time to banish negative voices and replace them with positive attitudes and affirmations. Let the imagination soar. If we can envision it, we can be it.

Affirmation
I learn new things by keeping an open mind.

Child of Fire

The Child of Fire laughs in delight at the flames of a campfire that dance and dazzle him. Humans have gazed into flames since the beginning of time, fascinated by the warmth, radiance, visions—and even danger—the fire brings. Yet all this is a wondrous discovery for each child who sees fire for the first time. His companion, the tabby cat, is as comfortable in the shadows as she is basking in the glow of the firelight.

When you get this card in a reading...
The Child of Fire is inspired and ready to make something happen! It's time to try something new. His enthusiasm makes him a joy to be around and his eagerness to take chances is contagious. This person probably learns best by doing and thinking "why not go for it?" There's a lot of laughter and playfulness coming into his life right now.

When you read the Shadow side of this card...
Someone may be in too much of a hurry to start a new project. He could be impetuous and a bit reckless. He might consider slowing down a little, paying more attention to the details, and thinking things through before he rushes in. On the other hand, he may be too serious and need more playfulness in his life.

Affirmation
I jump at new opportunities.

Child of Water

The Child of Water stands at the tideline, where the water meets the shore. As the tide flows and ebbs, treasures are uncovered then re-covered once more. The water's edge is a place of fascination and magic for children and adults alike. The Child points to a bright orange sea star she has discovered. Nearby, a hermit crab scuttles along, carrying its house on its back. All around her, rocks and shells are strewn like jewels. Sunlight sparkles on the water. Behind the child, Mama Ocean rises and falls, ebbs and flows, and the sound of her ripples and waves are a lullaby of the heart.

When you get this card in a reading...
The Child of Water is tender-hearted and dreamy, and has a rich imaginary life. She may be attracted to a new spiritual path or philosophy, or drawn to a new art medium. She may be experiencing love for the first time. She needs to embrace her emotions, dreams, and imagination, and let her heart be filled.

When you read the Shadow side of this card...
Someone may be overly sensitive or lost in a fantasy life. She could be disappointed by love, or afraid of opening up her heart. Se may have been deeply wounded as a child; if so, she is being nudged to find help and move into a place of healing.

Affirmation
I imagine a life filled with love, art, and spirituality.

Child of Earth

The Child of Earth holds a ripe apple in his small hands. It's fresh-picked, right off the tree, and its tangy aroma tickles the Child's nose. It feels heavy, solid, and grounding in his hands. He gazes at the apple as if it holds all the mysteries of the universe—and perhaps it does, for a pentacle of apple seeds is revealed when the apple is cut crossways. His companion, Rabbit, is most often seen in those borderline times of dawn and dusk, when it is easiest to slip between this world and the Otherworld.

When you get this card in a reading ...
The Child of Earth is fascinated by the natural world and is learning new ways to connect with it. Perhaps he is learning to sit still at a "secret spot" and observe the changes from day to day and season to season. Or perhaps he's decided to grow his own food. He may be concerned with health issues and is starting a new way of eating or a new exercise program. Or he may be learning how to take care of his money and other resources responsibly.

When you read the Shadow side of this card ...
Someone may be too attached to possessions and might be valuing others by how much they earn. He may have an unhealthy lifestyle and is resistant to change. He may prefer to stay indoors and let the natural world

pass him by. It's time to start fresh and begin a new relationship with the material world.

Affirmation
By connecting to my body and the natural world, I find my center.

Explorers

Seeking Challenges, Being Driven By a Quest

Each explorer is actively engaged with discovering the qualities of his or her suit. They are climbing high, spinning fire, surfing, or tracking wild animals. The explorers are at a time in their lives when they are investigating options, before they've chosen or discovered their life's path or passion.

The Explorers correspond to Knights in traditional decks. In readings, Explorers seek challenges and are driven by a quest or goal in areas associated with their element. They are full of youthful excitement and have the energy and courage to put things in motion. The Explorers are all young adults, in their twenties or thirties. In a life cycle, they represent the quality of growth, corresponding to a waxing first-quarter or gibbous moon. The Explorer cards can be read as another person, an aspect of yourself, or the quality of taking on a quest or energetically moving towards a goal.

Explorer of Air

The Explorer of Air climbs a tall tree in the woods. From this height he has a new perspective on the world—he can see what the birds see as he gazes out over the landscape. He carries quiver, bow, and blade with him, all tools of discernment and focus. He has studied and learned the language of the birds. He knows more than their songs; he also knows their companion and conflict calls, their begging and alarm calls. He understands when the birds tell each other about the deer laying quietly in the thicket, the fox silently watching, the hawk coming in to raid the songbird's nest for eggs. He knows too that birds can be messengers from the Otherworld, as they move back and forth between the world of Spirit and the physical world. His ally is Peregrine Falcon, a raptor who is in the process of recovering after nearly becoming extinct. Falcon offers the gifts of speed, grace, and mental agility.

When you get this card in a reading...
The Explorer of Air's ability to learn quickly serves him well. He is a skillful problem solver and strategist. His study of the language and habits of birds enables him to overlook the artificial boundaries humans have created. His bird's eye view shows him unity where others see separation, and helps him make longterm plans. He offers intuition and insight and is eager to investigate alternative ways of doing things. Rarely satisfied with the status quo, this card reveals someone who may be a

bit of a rebel or iconoclast, but who also loves to teach and share their knowledge.

When you read the Shadow side of this card...

Although intelligence and wit are important, sometimes these skills are used in an arrogant, hurtful way. In a rush to be right, far-reaching consequences can be ignored to one's peril. Take care that you aren't more concerned about your ideals or arguments than you are about others' experiences and feelings.

Affirmation

I climb high in order to get perspective and take the long view.

Explorer of Fire

The Explorer of Fire spins her flaming orbs through the darkness, making a pattern of dazzling light that arcs, loops, and falls. Her movements are as sensuous and sinuous as a serpent, and just as mesmerizing. She has practiced long hours to make her movements look effortless. But the skill of fire spinning requires her to be balanced, coordinated, flexible, and daring. She wears the mask of a fire goddess; in her trance state, perhaps she becomes one. As the flames whoosh around her, she enters the silence at the center of the circle. Fire dancers say that none of them ever escapes without being burned at least once. Fire consumes and transforms. It's dangerous, erotic, and hot. The fire spinner's ally is Salamander, who offers the gift of assisting us through our transformations and re-energizing us when life seems devoid of passion.

When you get this card in a reading...
Someone is "playing with fire." What fast-paced, high-energy situations are being ignited? Taking risks energizes. This is a chance to entertain and dazzle. Share your enthusiasm and let the sparks fly. Creativity and eroticism can revitalize something that has become stale.

The Explorer inspires others by taking a bold stand. She is willing to ignore possible danger, moving quickly and fearlessly on important issues she is passionate about. Be bold! Now is the time to take courageous action.

When you read the Shadow side of this card...
Find the still center in the midst of the fire dance. Beware of a volatile temper or situation. Someone may be headstrong, or lack self-discipline, making them more reckless than courageous. There could be a tendency to get charged up about something, only to let the fire fizzle when something or someone else comes along. Is the fastest or most exciting way necessarily the best way to move forward?

Affirmation
I dare to be transformed by the flames of passion and creativity.

Explorer of Water

Surfing can be a form of deep meditation, a way of stopping the mind from thinking. As in meditation, if the surfer tries too hard to control his mind, he becomes rigid and tight. The wave then overtakes him and he wipes out.

But the Explorer of Water knows how to be pulled into the present moment, hyper-aware and effortlessly concentrating. He dances on Mama Gaia's belly of water, the very essence of harmony and ease. He has found the sweet spot where all is effortless, moving with the wave that carries him with exquisite grace.

His ally is Dolphin, who offers the gifts of balance and harmony, and the wisdom of deep breathing.

When you get this card in a reading...
This is joy that comes from within—it is not dependent on outer circumstances. The Explorer of Water is romantic and charming, and others are drawn to the deep well of peace inside him. He loves yoga, meditation, and any of the mystical arts. He expresses his deep feelings and spirituality through art, music, or dance. He flows with great compassion for others, and imagines things as they could be.

When you read the Shadow side of this card...
There is a tendency to be lost in fantasies or emotional extremes. Someone may be addicted to substances or to the experience of the next spiritual "high," without

grounding it in the physical world. Someone may be feeling spiritually superior to others. Be careful about respecting other people's boundaries, and make sure you have strong boundaries of your own.

Affirmation

I am riding the deep waves of joy and peace in my life.

Explorer of Earth

The Explorer of Earth is a tracker, one who knows how to read the stories imprinted on the earth by the birds and animals who live there. Her awareness of the life of the forest is keen. She has been examining the duff at the base of the fir tree, looking for tracks or scat that might indicate what small creature has passed this way. Perhaps she has found the bones of a vole or songbird. She looks up quickly when her attention is caught by a scurrying squirrel. Perhaps he is letting her know about the buck who stands just behind her. Is he a spirit deer, or a rare white deer?

The Explorer of Earth knows how to live close to the heart of nature. She knows how to make primitive tools, to start a fire with a bow drill, to smoke and dry food for the winter, to make clothing from animal hides and to weave baskets from cedar bark. Living in the wilderness teaches her that she is capable of far more than she had ever thought. She does not fear the forest, but respects it and has become part of it. Her ally is Badger, who offers the gifts of stability, earth knowledge, and connection to home.

When you get this card in a reading…

The Explorer of Earth experiences her spirituality in her body and in her relationship with the earth. Although she is very realistic and practical, she is also very intuitive. This is a time to connect to the Great Mystery (God/dess) by spending time in nature. The

Explorer's spirituality is pragmatic, focused on the "how" of spiritual teachings, rather than the "why."

She has made an art of green, sustainable living, and has much to teach about the spiritual rewards of choosing simplicity. Follow her example and be cautious at this time with your money, spending it wisely and tracking its inflow and outgo. Repair and recycle what you can, rather than making new purchases. This is a time for finding pleasure in the rewards of hard work, especially if you are doing what comes easily and naturally to you. She also reminds us that staying fit and eating a wholesome diet are the best kind of health care.

When you read the Shadow side of this card …

This may be a time of disconnect from the natural world, with little interest in its mysteries and miracles. Unhappiness can come from living too much in the head or not paying attention to physical or financial matters. Someone may be overly cautious about taking needed risks, or is struggling with money problems. Pessimism and neglectful resource management reflect poor stewardship of the bounty with which Mama Gaia blesses us.

Affirmation

I live within Nature's bounty.

Guardians

Protecting and Nurturing the Community

Each Guardian nurtures and preserves the qualities of her or his suit. They tone with a singing bowl, tend the community fire, pour out offerings of ocean water, and gather in the harvest.

The Guardians correspond to Queens in traditional decks. In readings, Guardians are productive and actively involved in their communities. They "guard" or protect the qualities and issues defined by their suits. The Guardians are all at midlife, in their forties, fifties, or sixties. In a life cycle, they represent the quality of fruition, corresponding to a full or disseminating moon. The Guardian cards can be read as another person, an aspect of yourself, or the qualities of being nurturing, creative, productive, and fulfilled.

Guardian of Air

The Guardian of Air is a yogini whose bare feet don't feel the cold of the snow. Here is not a woman who puts up with pretensions or incompetence in others. Her challenging gaze pierces you like a knife. She looks straight into your soul, shining a light on even the dustiest corners. She has removed herself from mainstream society, preferring the starkness and solitude of a mountaintop. She has spent so much time in meditation and prayer that she has expanded her awareness to experience the entire cosmos. From this vantage point high in the mountains, as you listen to the toning of the singing bowl—what becomes crystal clear to you about your life? She guards and nurtures the qualities of communication, decision-making, strategy, prayer, and meditation. Her ally is Snowy Owl, who offers the gifts of prophecy, insight, and clarity—whether in full daylight or darkest night.

When you get this card in a reading…
The Guardian of Air brings clarity to every situation, even if it hurts. She sees straight through to the core of things, making her very candid and direct. She teaches us to cut away everything that is extraneous, until only the truth of the matter remains. She bestows gifts of skillful communication, whether writing, speaking, or editing. The Guardian of Air places great value on self-discipline and has little patience with those who do not. This may be reflected in an autonomous or austere

lifestyle. Now is not the time to shrink from making difficult decisions. It is time to speak the truth loudly, boldly, and with great integrity.

When you read the Shadow side of this card …

What needs to be said? What is preventing communication? Too many words (or too few) may be confusing the issue at hand. Someone who is very influential may be overly judgmental. It is easy to be critical of others, and care should be taken that wit does not become biting sarcasm. Tact and clarity are needed. The right word at the right moment is a precious jewel.

Affirmation

I declare my own truth with candor and clarity.

Guardian of Fire

This Guardian is a fire tender. He keeps an eye on the bonfire at festivals, making sure it neither gets too high nor gets so low that it goes out. His energy matches that of the fire, whether it's quiet, smoking, sparking, or blazing. He's often in the background of the circle, but the drumming and dancing can't happen without him. He's an integral part of the community. He guards and nurtures the qualities of creativity, personal power, passion, and transformation. His ally is Bobcat, who knows how to channel the life force silently but powerfully. Like the owl, he sees and hears clearly in the dark.

When you get this card in a reading...
The Guardian of Fire is someone who quietly knows his own worth. He doesn't have to be the center of attention in order to feel good about himself, although he is sometimes quite naturally in the spotlight. This is someone who attracts others because of a warm heart and natural radiance. Remember that when the flame of creativity is shared, all benefit, and no single fire is diminished. Passions shared and combined can create a bonfire big enough to light up the entire sky.

When you read the Shadow side of this card...
Someone may be demanding more attention than is appropriate. They may be full of ego and hogging the spotlight. What was a natural warmth may turn to anger. Behaving like a diva won't win many friends, and

jealousy of others' success is unworthy behavior. It is time to make allies with those whose good fortune is enviable.

Affirmation

I spark creativity in others while tending my own creative flame.

Guardian of Water

The Guardian of Water is calling us to open our hearts to compassion, intuition, and deep love. As if swimming in the waters of mercy, she overflows with forgiveness, peace, and cleansing for a troubled world. "Pour it out for me" is her siren song. A school of fish swirls all about her, as if they were her children or students, seeking comfort and closeness as they explore their world. The spiral *koru* necklace, echoed in the shape of the shell, signifies unfurling, opening, renewal. She guards and nurtures the qualities of intense emotions, dreams, and healing. Her ally is Sea Turtle, who offers the gifts of good luck, peace, longevity, and the ability to find our way home.

When you get this card in a reading...
The Guardian of Water is kind, gracious, and caring, with much empathy for those in need. Her love and compassion seem boundless, and she welcomes all in need of emotional comfort and mothering. She encourages a harmonious environment that may feature water, and teaches us to cleanse and refresh ourselves, especially after taking care of others. She guides us to cherish our dreams, follow our intuition, and listen to our hearts. Our feelings can be trusted to guide us.

When you read the Shadow side of this card...
There may be difficulty when the personal troubles of one person spill into those of others. Be wary of

people or situations that are overly needy or draining. Someone may be moody, self-indulgent, or impractical. Instead of wallowing in emotions, seek the patient, cleansing, forgiving powers of water, so that emotional balance may be restored.

Affirmation

I trust the waters of love and compassion flowing from my heart.

Guardian of Earth

The Guardian of Earth tenderly examines his corn to see if it is ripe for harvest. He has planted, tended, weeded, and nurtured the plants all season long. Now it's time to cut the corn and let it nourish his family and community. He takes great pride in his heirloom home-grown corn. He is reclaiming its sacred traditions, taking it back from giant agribusinesses who have commercialized and adulterated it. He guards and nurtures the qualities of good health, prosperity, security, practicality, and tradition. His ally is Horse, who offers the gifts of strength, power, and movement. Horse will help with the hard work of farming, yet also carry us on our journeys.

When you get this card in a reading...
The Guardian of Earth creates financial security and good health for himself and his family. He is a good steward of Gaia's resources. He builds wealth, not only for personal satisfaction and comfort, but also for the good work it can do in the world. This is a powerful person who can be depended on to provide a meal, a job, caretaking, or financial support. The tangible is much more appealing to him than the abstract. There is great benefit in being intimately aligned with the Earth.

When you read the Shadow side of this card...
Someone is being excessively conservative when it comes to money matters. Perhaps there is a reluctance

to share the hard-earned harvest with others. Or there may be trouble staying on a budget, with overindulgent spending. Care is needed to maintain good health, especially by eating healthier food. This is an important time to ground and center, and reconnect with the Earth.

Affirmation
I value good health and financial security, and enjoy providing for myself and my family.

Elders

Holding Wisdom, Giving Counsel

Each Elder passes on the wisdom and teachings of his or her suit. They play peaceful music, practice the arts of healing and magic, listen to the dawn's secrets, and transform wool into yarn.

The Elders correspond to Kings in traditional decks. In readings, Elders give counsel and take the long view. They are concerned with the wisdom of the ancestors as well as preparing the way for descendants yet to come. The Elders are all seventy years or older. In a life cycle, they represent the qualities of dissemination and release, corresponding to a third quarter or balsamic moon. The Elder cards can be read as another person, an aspect of yourself, or the quality of being an authority figure or counselor, setting an example for others.

Elder of Air

Can you hear the sweet sound rising from the aromatic cedar flute? A grandfather's prayer of thanksgiving wafts to the heavens as his breath becomes melody and harmony. This is a man who has dedicated his life to bringing peace and healing through music. The medicine of music creates a sanctuary for those in physical or spiritual pain, and stirs others to make a difference in the world. His ally Luna Moth flies high, carrying messages to and from the ancestors.

When you get this card in a reading...
The Elder of Air's message is echoed in the words of Frederick Buechner, that "vocation is the place where your deep gladness meets the world's deep need." He shows us how to experience communion with the Great Mystery through worship, praise, or meditation. He sets an example of a life well-lived. This is a time for making decisions, but if they affect others, make sure they are made ethically, with fairness to all.

The Elder of Air offers the gift of inspiration, balance, and clarity. His music can create a sacred space where deep wisdom and enlightenment are accessible.

When you read the Shadow side of this card...
Loneliness, self-pity, or even illness can cause someone to forget how to commune with the wisdom of the world. Forgetting may lead to headaches, forgetfulness, or even memory loss. A sense of isolation or being cut

off from others may be in play, possibly encouraging someone to cultivate an aura of mystery for ego reasons, making matters worse. However, music or an emphasis on fairness may restore spirits.

Affirmation
I am a song of peace and healing for the world.

Elder of Fire

A *curandera* (healer) squats on the earth in front of an altar honoring the ancestors during Los Días de los Muertos—the Days of the Dead. She holds a handful of burning herbs that direct waves of energy to dissipate the foul and bring in the sweet. She lives in *la época del mito* (the time of myth, the Otherworld) as much—or more—than she does in the world of consensual reality. Her gaze, directed at the viewer, is potent and challenging. She reminds us to open up to the Otherworld—the world of energy patterns, spirits, and invisibles. When we shift our inner reality, our outer reality shifts as well. Her ally is Iguana, who brings the medicine of the dreamtime.

When you get this card in a reading...
The Elder of Fire doesn't sit back and accept things as they are. She embodies the power of transformation. With her gifts of the shamanic and healing arts, she may use charms, spells, and incantations to facilitate needed change. But she is equally likely to use a pen, paintbrush, or a spoon and old cookpot.

This is someone whose vitality, pride, dignity, and accomplishments are powerfully attractive. But they can intimidate as well. There is currently a chance to slip between this world and the Otherworld, moving power and creativity back and forth between the two. Make things happen!

When you read the Shadow side of this card...
Beware of someone who is pushy, arrogant, and self-important. The person may behave like the proverbial snake oil salesman, promising miracles but failing to deliver. Dishonor may bring jealousy or vengeance. Someone who has ambitions to be a leader may be thwarted. There may be a temptation to practice a form of unethical magic. What will you do to bring yourself back into balance?

Affirmation
I am at home in all the worlds of power and transformation.

Elder of Water

A fisherman, who is intimately familiar with the tides and moods of Mother Ocean, rows his skiff out into the sound just before sunrise. It's a liminal time and place: between night and day, between shore and sea. His attention is caught by a water bird—a heron? eagle? cormorant?—and he looks up, his gaze full of wonder. As he feels the shifting current below him, he remembers a poem by Rumi: "The breeze at dawn has secrets to tell. Don't go back to sleep." His ally is Harbor Seal, who is comfortable swimming above and below the water. Seal reminds us to pay attention to our dreams as they arise from the deep, and to be at home in both our inner and outer worlds.

When you get this card in a reading…

The Elder of Water has had a lifelong practice of seeking out the wild and liminal places in Nature. This has given him a deep peacefulness in his soul and the ability to remain calm in the midst of turbulent emotions. Others seek out his comforting presence. This is someone known for his kindness, and his ability to deeply listen, especially to those in crisis.

The Elder of Water reminds us that to some degree, we each have a mission to be of service to others. Upon rising each day, we can bring the mysteries of our dreams into the light of day. In the evenings, if we reflect on the day just passed, we can live in a state of endless gratitude.

When you read the Shadow side of this card ...
There may be someone who is hiding or stuffing their feelings, or a situation where emotions are being hidden. Is someone telling people what they want to hear? Perhaps they are having difficulty saying no. Beware of someone who would take advantage of others in need of help by exerting unhealthy control over them. Someone may be self-delusional or lost in a sea of emotions. In what ways might giving thanks or reconnecting to the wild restore peace?

Affirmation
I seek out the wild and magical places that fill my heart with gratitude.

Elder of Earth

A woman sits in her lush autumnal garden, spinning wool into yarn that will eventually become sweaters, scarves, and hats for the winter to come. She is an industrious woman who has tended her orchard all year long and now reaps a rich harvest of apples. She shares the windfalls with Sister Deer, an original inhabitant of the land. Deer speaks of the Elder's gentleness and strength. She is content to spin out her days in harmony with her place and her community. Spinsters throughout the ages have been known for their magical abilities to spin straw into gold, to open doorways between the worlds, and to control the destiny of women and men. She reminds us of the Three Fates: She Who Spins, She Who Weaves, and She Who Cuts the Thread of Life. She will play each of those roles in turn, but as for today, she spins.

When you get this card in a reading...

The Elder of Earth lives a simple but abundant life. Her hard work and diligence have created wealth, and she enjoys ample security and stability. Yet she knows that true prosperity lies in her relationship with the land, family, friends, and community, and with the Great Mystery. She lives the truth that these are riches beyond measure.

There is great wisdom in a lifestyle of simplicity and self-sufficiency, and cultivating these skills can enrich all. This is someone who may have earned community recognition and respect, thanks to a lifetime of dedicated work on behalf of Mama Gaia, for instance, by championing environmental issues. The Elder of Earth is deeply content within, at peace with her place in the world.

When you read the Shadow side of this card ...
Someone may be miserly and refusing to share their bounty with others. This is not the way of Mother Earth's abundance and diversity, nor is rigidity and resistance to the need for change or growth. Beware of any failure to take care of family or the land. Perhaps there is someone who seems dazzled by luxury possessions, or who is seeking to prove their worth by showing off their wealth. The Elder of Earth shows us the contentment of recognizing what comprises true value and worth.

Affirmation
I spin a prosperous and abundant life for myself and those I love.

Working with the Cards

Whether it's by yourself or with someone else, when you sit down to do a reading, it's always a good idea to ground and center first with deep breathing. You can establish sacred space by lighting a candle or a stick of incense, or using another method. I like to use a special reading cloth a friend made for me. It's beautiful and sensual, and I don't use it for anything else. Even if I lay it down on top of a messy desk, it's a signal to my subconscious that we have moved into "sacred time."

Shuffle in any way that feels comfortable to you. If you are using large cards, it's easier to lay them out on a cloth and mix them up, rather than trying to shuffle them in your hands. Focus intently on your question as you shuffle, and keep going until you feel like you're done. I like to cut the deck with my non-dominant hand. You'll find the shuffling and cutting ritual that works best for you.

Reading the Cards Intuitively

Almost everyone starts to play with a new deck by laying cards out in a spread, then looking up the meaning of the cards in the companion book. There's nothing wrong with that approach; it's definitely a good idea to know why the deck creator chose certain elements and symbols for each card. But you are not limited to the deck creator's interpretations. You need to develop your own. Trust your own intuition and responses to the cards. Here's a few ideas for intuitively reading the cards.

- Simply describe the card, as if you were describing it to another person. Use lots of adjectives and descriptive phrases. What is going on? How do the figures seem to feel in this situation? What is the card's atmosphere?
- Ask yourself: What does the card look like? What does it remind me of? Notice your first impressions, and your emotional reaction to the card. Love it? Hate it? Puzzled by it?
- Throw out a few one-word descriptions (like "serene" "innocent" "peaceful").
- Give it a title ("Woman in the Water").
- Be open to wild ideas or associations that fly into your head.

Jot down your impressions of the card before you look up the meaning in the book. Then compare your own impressions to the description in the book. What unique insights do you have?

A Card a Day

When you are getting to know a new deck like this one, one of the best things you can do is pull a card a day. Look at the card closely, and take note of all the details, colors, and patterns. Meditate on it and write a brief journal entry about the thoughts and associations it brings up for you. Think about how it applies to your own life. The card will then come alive for you, and its meaning will expand far beyond the descriptions I have written in this book.

If you like, you can ask a question before you turn up a card, like these:

- What do I need to keep in mind today?
- What wisdom does this card offer me today?
- What might this card have to teach me about having a successful, happy day?

If you can, keep the card propped up so you'll see it all day by your computer or on your desk or altar.

The Art of Asking Questions

Often, you or the person you're reading for won't know exactly what question they want to ask. You know you are troubled by a situation, or want some guidance, but are vague about specific questions. Take as long as you need to clarify your question. Fuzzy questions will generally lead to fuzzy answers.

It is helpful to focus on the area of life you're interested in (such as relationships, career, health, money, travel, spiritual paths) and the time frame (right now, within the next week, month, season, or year). I have found the most success in doing readings for short periods of time. Doing a reading for a year from now may not give you accurate results, as the future is not set in stone.

It's best to ask open-ended questions that begin with "What," "How," or "Where" rather than "Will XYZ happen?" Open-ended questions are much more empowering and insightful than yes/no questions.

Mary K. Greer has said that her favorite all-purpose question is: "What do I most need to look at in my life right now?" and I agree. Sometimes I add a topic, so the question becomes: "What do I most need to know about my health right now?" or "What do I most need to know about my primary relationship right now?"

Three-Card Readings

I love three-card readings. I find that you can often go directly to the heart of a matter much more quickly than when you lay out a spread with ten or more cards. Here are several examples of placements for three-card readings:

- 1 - Opportunity
  2 - Challenge
  3 - Resolution (or Possible Outcome)

- 1 - Past: some experience in the past that has helped shape the current situation.
  2 - Present: what is going on right now.
  3 - Future: where the querent or situation is heading.

- 1 - Mind: your intellectual attitudes.
  2 - Body: your actions.
  3 - Spirit: a lesson you can learn from the situation.

More Spreads

Here are some of my favorite spreads. I created some of them and others were created by some of my favorite tarot readers. Enjoy!

James Wells' Helpful All-Purpose Spread

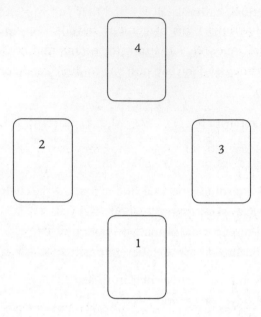

1. *Now.* What's going on? The present energies or circumstances of the topic or situation.

2. *Helpful action(s).* Things appropriate to do or embody in this situation. Positive doable step(s). This placement can also be read as: helpful people, situations, or opportunities. (You can pull one to three cards for this step.)

3. *What to avoid.* Things that would not be helpful or constructive in this situation. What not to do. Negative actions. This placement can also be read as: pitfalls; people, situations, or events that could be detrimental. (You can pull one to three cards for this step.)

4. *Most Likely Outcome.* Depends on whatever time frame(s) you and/or the querent decide. Timeline: if you pull one card, ask the querent the time frame (three months, six months, a year). If you pull two or more cards, assign a time frame to each. Or do one card per month for the allotted time frame. For example: three cards signifying 3 months, 6 months, 1 year.

For example, if you only lay out one card for position 4, the querent decides what time frame it covers (usually three months). Or if you lay out three cards for position 4, can represent three time intervals, such as three months, six months, and a year. Or, if the querent wants to explore the next four months, you could lay out four cards—one for each month.

(©2010 James Wells. Used with permission. See "Circle Ways," http://jameswells.wordpress.com/)

Beth Owl's Daughter's "Predict Your Future By Creating It" Spread

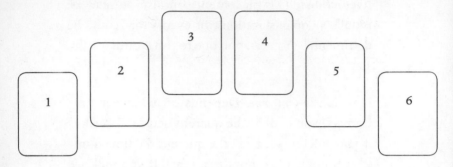

Beth first separates the major arcana cards from the rest of the deck. From the majors, she asks her client to look through them face up and choose two. One will represent how they feel about or would describe their current situation, and the other represents where they wish to be. She says, "Because it can be hard to narrow down one's favorites from all the beautiful possibilities, I've found that if they go through and first discard the ones that don't fit at all, then make a subset of their 'semi-finalists,' it's easier for them to finally settle on the ones they want. And they always amaze me with their wise, powerful choices! Even (sometimes especially) when they have no prior knowledge of the tarot."

Beth then shuffles the deck thoroughly, mixing the majors back in with the rest of the deck. The client then chooses four cards, face down. These are placed between the two face-up majors they chose.

Card 1 (Client's face up chosen major): Where you are today.

Card 2: (First card, chosen face down) What challenges you.

Card 3: (Second face down card) What action you can take to meet this challenge.

Card 4: (Third face down card) The next step.

Card 5: (Fourth face down card) How does Mystery help you?

Card 6 (Client's face up chosen major): Outcome/ Where you want to be.

(©2010 Beth Owl's Daughter. Used with permission. See "Beth Owl's Daughter: Practical Wisdom for Extraordinary Living," http://www.owlsdaughter.com)

James Wells' Ten Card Layout
(An alternative to the Celtic Cross layout)

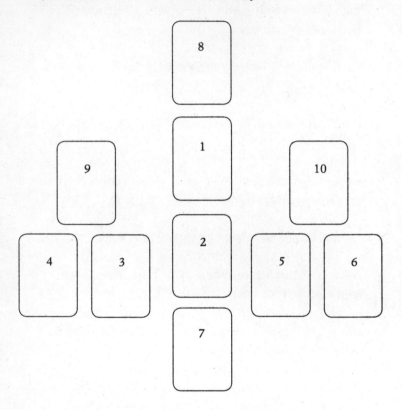

1. My external experience of the situation.

2. My internal experience of the situation.

3. My contribution to the situation.

4. Other(s)'s contribution to the situation.

5. Challenges, blocks, or problems connected with the situation.

6. Blessings, gifts, or resources connected with the situation.

7. What Soul—the Personal Sacred or the Sacred Self—has to say about the situation. *

8. What Spirit—the Transpersonal Sacred or the Sacred Other has to say about the situation. **

9. The wisdom that can emerge for me from this situation. What I can learn from it.

10. Based on the above information, how this situation will most likely unfold by [chosen time frame].

(©2010 James Wells. Used with permission. See "Circle Ways," http://jameswells.wordpress.com/)

Joanna's New Moon Spread

To be done at each new moon.

How can I best seed the energy of this new moon to bring me into deeper personal wisdom?

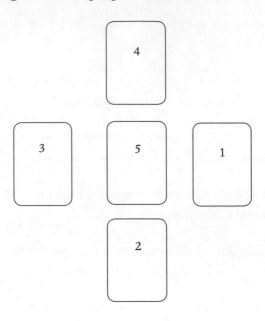

1. How can I best seed the energy of this new moon in the East (in communication, thought, information, intention, meditation)?

2. How can I best seed the energy of this new moon in the South (in passion, creativity, energy, sexuality, personal power)?

3. How can I best seed the energy of this new moon in the West (in emotions, intuition, dreams, sensuality, compassion)?

4. How can I best seed the energy of this new moon in the North (in stability, security, health, finances, manifestation)?

5. How can I best seed the energy of this new moon in the center (in my connection to Spirit)?

Check in on it each week to see how it's manifesting during the month. Do a little journal writing, even if it's just notes, once a week. See how it blossoms at the full moon and releases its seeds for the next cycle during the waning moon, turning into compost at the dark.

Joanna's New Moon Spread 2

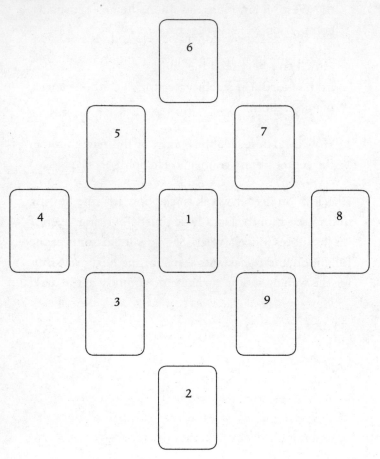

1. Seed of This New Moon: what seed begins to grow this new moon?

2. The Querent: how do you behave and respond during this lunation to the issues the moon illuminates for you?

3. The Challenge: what is the central challenge of this lunation?

4. Last Lunation: what is now passing away from the last lunation?

5. Waxing Moon: what grows as the moon waxes?

6. Full Moon: what peaks as the moon becomes full?

7. Waning Moon: what do you let go of or surrender as the moon wanes?

8. Lessons: what are the key lessons of this lunation?

9. Seed of the Next New Moon: what seed will begin to grow during the next lunation? (This card will become Card 1 of next month's reading.)

Joanna's New Year Spread

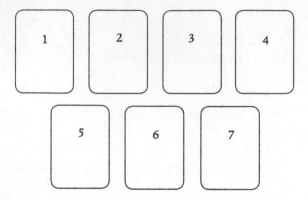

This reading should be done around the new year.

1. What do I leave behind in the old year?

2. What do I open up to in the new year?

3. Key opportunity of the new year

4. Key challenge of the new year

5. Hidden concern (pull from bottom of the deck)

6. Deep Wisdom / Advice from God/dess (pull from middle of the deck)

7. Key theme of the new year

If you keep records of your readings, the last card (7) could become the first card (1) in next year's spread.

Carolyn Cushing's "Aligning with the Earth" Spread

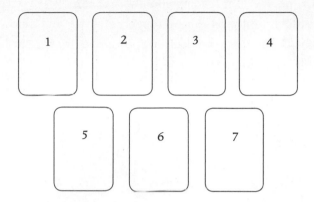

WISDOM READING (INSPIRED BY RACHEL POLLACK'S WORK):

1. What is the earth teaching humanity now?

2. What have we (humanity) already learned and need to use?

3. What is our next area of growth?

4. How do we make the leap between what we know and how we need to grow?

   PERSONAL READING:

5. What is my role in helping humanity to make the leap?

6. What do I already know and need to share?

7. What is my next area of growth?

This spread can be powerful using two decks—one for the Wisdom reading and another for the Personal reading—as cards can be repeated above and below. The Gaian Tarot is especially appropriate for the earth-focused Wisdom reading.

(©2010 Carolyn Cushing. Used with permission. See "Art of Change Tarot," http://artofchangetarot.wordpress.com/)

James Wells' Gaian Spread

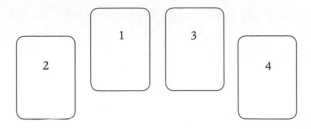

This layout is based on the idea of a reciprocal relationship with Gaia, our mother the earth. It's appropriate at any time, but particularly apt on Earth Day or on any of the equinoxes, solstices, or cross-quarter days. Use any insights you receive from your reading to create concrete actions so that you make a difference in your own life and in the life of creation of which we are a part. It's best not to do this layout again until you've incorporated the wisdom of the current reading and performed some actions, even small ones, to embody that wisdom.

1. What does Gaia need from me at this time?

2. How can I offer this to her?

3. What do I need from Gaia at this time?

4. How can I receive this from her?

(©2010 James Wells. Used with permission. See "Circle Ways," http://jameswells.wordpress.com/)

Bibliography

Andrews, Ted. *Animal-Speak: The Spiritual & Magical Powers of Creatures Great & Small*. St. Paul, MN: Llewellyn, 1996.

———. *Animal-Wise: The Spirit Language and Signs of Nature*. Jackson, TN: Dragonhawk, 1999.

Austen, Hallie Iglehart. *The Heart of the Goddess*. Berkeley, CA: Wingbow Press, 1990.

Baldwin, Christina. *The Seven Whispers: A Spiritual Practice for Times Like These*. Novato, CA: New World Library, 2002.

Banzhaf, Hajo. *Tarot and the Journey of the Hero*. York Beach, ME: Samuel Weiser, 2000.

Bruce-Mitford, Miranda. *The Illustrated Book of Signs & Symbols*. New York: DK Publishing Inc., 1996.

Chevalier, Jean. *The Penguin Dictionary of Symbols*. New York: Penguin, 1997.

Chisholm, Chris. *Wolf Journey: Part One, Trail of the Naturalist*. Bellingham, WA: Wolf Camp, 1996.

Estes, Clarissa Pinkola. *Women Who Run With the Wolves*. New York: Ballantine Books, 1992.

Fontana, David. *The Secret Language of Symbols*. San Francisco: Chronicle Books, 1993.

Gadon, Elinor. *The Once and Future Goddess: A Symbol for Our Time*. San Francisco: Harper & Row, 1989.

George, Demetra. *Mysteries of the Dark Moon*. San Francisco: Harper, 1992.

Gimbutas, Marija. *The Language of the Goddess*. San Francisco: Harper, 1995.

Greer, Mary K. *21 Ways to Read a Tarot Card*. St. Paul, MN: Llewellyn, 2006.

———. *The Complete Book of Tarot Reversals*. St. Paul, MN: Llewellyn, 2002.

Greer, Mary K., and Tom Tadfor Little. *Understanding the Tarot Court*. St. Paul, MN: Llewellyn, 2004.

Johnson, Buffie. *Lady of the Beasts: The Goddess and Her Sacred Animals*. San Francisco: Harper & Row, 1988.

Matthews, Daniel. *Cascade-Olympic Natural History: A Trailside Reference*. Seattle: Raven Editions, 1992.

McElroy, Mark. *Absolute Beginners Guide to Tarot*. Indianapolis: Que, 2006.

Michelsen, Teresa. *The Complete Tarot Reader: Everything You Need to Know from Start to Finish*. St. Paul, MN: Llewellyn, 2005.

National Audubon Society Regional Guide to the Pacific Northwest. New York: Knopf, 1998.

Pojar, Jim, and Andy MacKinnon. *Plants of the Pacific Northwest Coast: Washington, Oregon, British Columbia, and Alaska*. Auburn, WA: Lone Pine, 1994.

Pollack, Rachel. *The Complete Illustrated Guide to Tarot*. Boston: Element Books, 1999.

———. *The Forest of Souls: A Walk Through the Tarot*. St. Paul, MN: Llewellyn, 2002.

———. *Rachel Pollack's Tarot Wisdom: Spiritual Teachings and Deeper Meanings*. St. Paul, MN: Llewellyn, 2008.

Tanner, Wilda B. *The Mystical Magical Marvelous World of Dreams*. Tahlequah, OK: Sparrow Hawk Press, 1988.

Thomson, Sandra A. *Pictures from the Heart: A Tarot Dictionary*. New York: St. Martin's Griffin, 2003.

Young, Jon, Ellen Haas, and Evan McGown. *Coyote's Guide to Connecting with Nature for Kids of All Ages and Their Mentors*. Shelton, WA: OWLink Media, 2008.

To Write to the Author

If you wish to contact the author or would like more information about this book, please write to the author in care of Llewellyn Worldwide and we will forward your request. Both the author and publisher appreciate hearing from you and learning of your enjoyment of this book and how it has helped you. Llewellyn Worldwide cannot guarantee that every letter written to the author can be answered, but all will be forwarded. Please write to:

Joanna Powell Colbert
℅ Llewellyn Worldwide
2143 Wooddale Drive
Woodbury, MN 55125-2989

Please enclose a self-addressed stamped envelope for reply, or $1.00 to cover costs. If outside the U.S.A., enclose an international postal reply coupon.